Terminal Illness

Opposing Viewpoints®

Other Books of Related Interest

Terminal Illness

Opposing Viewpoints®

Mary E. Williams, *Book Editor*

David L. Bender, *Publisher*
Bruno Leone, *Executive Editor*
Bonnie Szumski, *Editorial Director*
Stuart B. Miller, *Managing Editor*

**OPPOSING
VIEWPOINTS®
SERIES**

Greenhaven Press, Inc., San Diego, California

Cover photo: PhotoDisc

Library of Congress Cataloging-in-Publication Data

Terminal illness : opposing viewpoints / Mary E. Williams, book
    editor.
        p.   cm. — (Opposing viewpoints series)
    Includes bibliographical references and index.
    ISBN 0-7377-0525-6 (pbk. : alk. paper) —
ISBN 0-7377-0526-4 (lib. bdg. : alk. paper)
    1. Terminal care. 2. Terminal care—Miscellanea.
3. Death—Miscellanea. 4. Right to die—Miscellanea.
5. Euthanasia—Miscellanea. I. Williams, Mary E., 1960–   .
II. Series: Opposing viewpoints series (Unnumbered)

R726.8 .T4646 2001
362.1'75—dc21   00-056044
                                                                      CIP

Greenhaven Press, Inc., P.O. Box 289009
San Diego, CA 92198-9009

> "Congress shall make no law. . . abridging the freedom of speech, or of the press."

First Amendment to the U.S. Constitution

The basic foundation of our democracy is the First Amendment guarantee of freedom of expression. The Opposing Viewpoints Series is dedicated to the concept of this basic freedom and the idea that it is more important to practice it than to enshrine it.

Contents

Why Consider Opposing Viewpoints?

"The only way in which a human being can make some approach to knowing the whole of a subject is by hearing what can be said about it by persons of every variety of opinion and studying all modes in which it can be looked at by every character of mind. No wise man ever acquired his wisdom in any mode but this."

John Stuart Mill

In our media-intensive culture it is not difficult to find differing opinions. Thousands of newspapers and magazines and dozens of radio and television talk shows resound with differing points of view. The difficulty lies in deciding which opinion to agree with and which "experts" seem the most credible. The more inundated we become with differing opinions and claims, the more essential it is to hone critical reading and thinking skills to evaluate these ideas. Opposing Viewpoints books address this problem directly by presenting stimulating debates that can be used to enhance and teach these skills. The varied opinions contained in each book examine many different aspects of a single issue. While examining these conveniently edited opposing views, readers can develop critical thinking skills such as the ability to compare and contrast authors' credibility, facts, argumentation styles, use of persuasive techniques, and other stylistic tools. In short, the Opposing Viewpoints Series is an ideal way to attain the higher-level thinking and reading skills so essential in a culture of diverse and contradictory opinions.

In addition to providing a tool for critical thinking, Opposing Viewpoints books challenge readers to question their own strongly held opinions and assumptions. Most people form their opinions on the basis of upbringing, peer pressure, and personal, cultural, or professional bias. By reading carefully balanced opposing views, readers must directly confront new ideas as well as the opinions of those with whom they disagree. This is not to simplistically argue that everyone who reads opposing views will—or should—change his or her opinion. Instead, the series enhances readers' understanding of their own views by encouraging confrontation with opposing ideas. Careful examination of others' views can lead to the readers' understanding of the logical inconsistencies in their own opinions, perspective on why they hold an opinion, and the consideration of the possibility that their opinion requires further evaluation.

Evaluating Other Opinions

To ensure that this type of examination occurs, Opposing Viewpoints books present all types of opinions. Prominent spokespeople on different sides of each issue as well as well-known professionals from many disciplines challenge the reader. An additional goal of the series is to provide a forum for other, less known, or even unpopular viewpoints. The opinion of an ordinary person who has had to make the decision to cut off life support from a terminally ill relative, for example, may be just as valuable and provide just as much insight as a medical ethicist's professional opinion. The editors have two additional purposes in including these less known views. One, the editors encourage readers to respect others' opinions—even when not enhanced by professional credibility. It is only by reading or listening to and objectively evaluating others' ideas that one can determine whether they are worthy of consideration. Two, the inclusion of such viewpoints encourages the important critical thinking skill of objectively evaluating an author's credentials and bias. This evaluation will illuminate an author's reasons for taking a particular stance on an issue and will aid in readers' evaluation of the author's ideas.

As series editors of the Opposing Viewpoints Series, it is our hope that these books will give readers a deeper understanding of the issues debated and an appreciation of the complexity of even seemingly simple issues when good and honest people disagree. This awareness is particularly important in a democratic society such as ours in which people enter into public debate to determine the common good.

Those with whom one disagrees should not be regarded as enemies but rather as people whose views deserve careful examination and may shed light on one's own.

Thomas Jefferson once said that "difference of opinion leads to inquiry, and inquiry to truth." Jefferson, a broadly educated man, argued that "if a nation expects to be ignorant and free . . . it expects what never was and never will be." As individuals and as a nation, it is imperative that we consider the opinions of others and examine them with skill and discernment. The Opposing Viewpoints Series is intended to help readers achieve this goal.

David L. Bender & Bruno Leone,
Series Editors

Greenhaven Press anthologies primarily consist of previously published material taken from a variety of sources, including periodicals, books, scholarly journals, newspapers, government documents, and position papers from private and public organizations. These original sources are often edited for length and to ensure their accessibility for a young adult audience. The anthology editors also change the original titles of these works in order to clearly present the main thesis of each viewpoint and to explicitly indicate the opinion presented in the viewpoint. These alterations are made in consideration of both the reading and comprehension levels of a young adult audience. Every effort is made to ensure that Greenhaven Press accurately reflects the original intent of the authors included in this anthology.

Introduction

"One of the greatest fears of a dying patient is not death, but the pain associated with the final days of life."
—*R. Henry Capps Jr., medical student, East Carolina University School of Medicine*

William Bergman, a retired railroad detective from Hayward, California, was diagnosed with terminal lung cancer in February 1998. According to his daughter, Beverly, Bergman's two final wishes were to be free of pain and to live out the rest of his days at home with his family. Although Bergman arranged a release from the hospital and a return to his home, the drugs his internist prescribed for pain were largely ineffective. "He died at home," states Beverly Bergman, "but in miserable pain."

Beverly Bergman filed a complaint with the Medical Board of California, asking that her father's physician be penalized for failing to prescribe stronger drugs that could have alleviated the dying man's pain. While the board agreed that Mr. Bergman had received inadequate pain treatment, no disciplinary actions were taken.

The Bergman case exemplifies a recent trend in health care advocacy. As *New York Times* reporter Sheryl Stolberg writes,

> For decades, doctors have worried that they might be disciplined, or even face criminal prosecution, for the aggressive use of morphine and other narcotics to control pain. Now, some advocates are trying to swing the pendulum in the other direction, by pressing authorities to punish doctors for not using pain medicine aggressively enough.

Doctors' wariness about administering pain-killing opiates is understandable, commentators point out. In an attempt to curb drug trafficking and narcotics abuse and addiction, many states require physicians to keep detailed records of prescriptions for controlled substances. Dr. Wing Chin, William Bergman's internist, lives in a state where special prescription pads are required for the administering of certain drugs. The pads make copies in triplicate—one for the doctor, one for the pharmacist, and one for drug enforcement officials. Chin maintains that when Beverly Bergman requested narcotics for her dying father, he was unable to quickly comply because he did not have the special pad with him. Instead, Chin prescribed a milder pain reliever that did not fall under the triplicate requirement.

Such occurrences reveal a need for the medical and legal communities to re-evaluate attitudes and policies that can result in the undertreatment of pain in the terminally ill, patients' advocates argue. "Terminally ill patients are in special situations," contends R. Henry Capps Jr., a medical student at East Carolina University. "Clearly, pain control is far more important for them than a nebulous avoidance of potentially harmful properties of pain medication."

Physicians' fears about overprescribing narcotics are not the only reasons that dying people often receive inadequate pain treatment, health care experts claim. The mainstream medical community in the United States has a tendency to emphasize "curing" over therapeutic "healing," critics argue. A patient's cure is perceived as success, while a patient's death is seen as a medical failure. Since a terminal patient cannot be cured, efforts to heal their pain are often halfhearted because the patient's impending death is considered a medical defeat.

Patients' advocates point out, moreover, that many of today's doctors and nurses acquired little or no training in end-of-life care while they were students. According to Ira Byock, president of the American Academy of Hospice and Palliative Medicine, education in end-of-life care is "woefully insufficient because it is often taught in electives, or given only small amounts of time within the standard curriculum." Just six out of the 125 medical schools in the United States offer a separate course in death and dying, and only 24 percent of the leading medical textbooks provide helpful information about end-of-life issues, reports the Robert Wood Johnson Foundation. One survey of a New York hospital found that almost all the medical residents who had had their first experience telling a patient about a terminal diagnosis had never witnessed a senior physician engage in such a conversation. Byock insists that medical curricula must change so that future standards of care for the dying will be more compassionate. In his opinion, "education about how to care for people when they're dying should be proportional to the amount of time devoted to obstetrics in medical and nursing schools."

In response to the calls for improvement in terminal care, a few medical schools and teaching hospitals have begun to offer more training in end-of-life issues. Some medical curricula are devoting more attention to palliative care, a medical specialization in the care of patients with incurable illnesses. Palliative-care physicians and nurses are trained to relieve pain and other symptoms associated with serious illness; they also address the psychological, emotional, and spiritual aspects of chronic and fatal disease. Such issues are capturing the interest of a growing number of medical students, palliative-care supporters maintain. One elective course in end-of-life care at Harvard, offered since 1994, is regularly oversubscribed and receives accolades from student evaluators. In 1999, New York's Mount Sinai School of Medicine opened a new Institute of Palliative Care. And in the year 2000, the U.S. Medical Licensing Exam included updated questions on palliative care. Proponents hope that this burst of interest in palliation and end-of-life issues will herald a new era of merciful care for the terminally ill.

Pain management for the dying is just one of many issues surrounding the care of the terminally ill that have arisen in recent years. Conflicting opinions about life support technologies, living wills, and physician-assisted suicide are also generating heated debate among health care experts and medical ethicists. *Terminal Illness: Opposing Viewpoints* explores these controversies in the following chapters: How Can Care of the Terminally Ill Be Improved? How Should the Physical and Emotional Pain of Terminal Illness Be Addressed? Should Physicians Be Permitted to Hasten the Deaths of Terminally Ill Patients? Do the Terminally Ill Have the Right to Die? The various answers to these questions present a compelling overview of the complex and difficult challenges faced by the fatally ill.

CHAPTER 1

How Can Care of the Terminally Ill Be Improved?

Chapter Preface

People diagnosed with terminal illnesses are confronted with painful and difficult choices. They must make decisions about potentially life-prolonging treatments, expensive medicines, experimental therapies, legal questions concerning life support and the right to die, and emotional issues affecting their family and loved ones.

One medical option for the dying that has received growing support in recent years is hospice care. Hospices employ the combined expertise of doctors, nurses, social workers, and counselors to focus on the physical, psychological, and spiritual needs of the dying patient. Hospice specialists, who may work in a residential facility or in a home, use various therapies to treat pain, depression, fatigue, and other debilitating symptoms associated with terminal illness. According to the National Hospice Organization, the hospice movement seeks neither "to hasten [death] nor to postpone it," but rather to "maximize the quality of remaining life through the provision of palliative [pain-relieving] therapies."

The hospice concept may be held in high regard, but many terminally ill patients are unable to take advantage of it. For one thing, doctors rarely inform their dying patients about hospices because most of them received little or no medical school training about end-of-life care. Furthermore, Medicare and private health insurance plans usually restrict hospice services to the last six months of life—even though recent advances in treatment have made it more difficult for doctors to predict when patients will die. In 1996, the Department of Health and Human Services reprimanded several large hospices for retaining patients who had survived beyond the six-month limit. The result, maintains hospice advocate Marilyn Webb, is that some doctors "are not referring patients for hospice care because they fear misestimating the time until death," and "hospices themselves are wary of taking certain patients for fear they will live too long."

The benefits and limitations of hospice care are among the issues taken up in the following chapter, which examines how society can best meet the needs of the fatally ill.

"Hospice . . . can make dying a time of psychological and spiritual growth in the very midst of sadness and loss."

Hospice Care Benefits the Terminally Ill

Marilyn Webb

In the following viewpoint, Marilyn Webb describes the benefits of hospice, a health care philosophy and practice that attends to the physical, psychological, and spiritual needs of the dying. Hospice workers—who may work in a residential facility or in a home—focus on alleviating the physical pain of terminal illness; they also help individuals face an impending death and achieve a psychological closure to life. The value of such assistance for the dying, Webb points out, has been largely ignored by the mainstream medical community. Webb is the author of *The Good Death: The New American Search to Reshape the End of Life*, from which this viewpoint is excerpted.

As you read, consider the following questions:
1. According to Sister Loretta, cited by the author, why do some dying patients often resist death?
2. When did the hospice movement begin in the United States?
3. In the opinion of Dr. Cicely Saunders, quoted by Webb, what is the "real work of dying"?

Excerpted from Marilyn Webb, *The Good Death: The New American Search to Reshape the End of Life*. Reprinted with permission from Bantam Books.

One night at the inpatient unit of Cabrini Hospice in Manhattan, Sister Loretta Palamara walked into a room to sit with a patient. "Joseph was actively dying," she later told me. "A young doctor—a new resident—was standing near him. Joseph had signed papers requesting no treatment. The young doctor didn't know what to do, since medically he'd done everything he *could* do."

Sister Loretta pulled a chair up next to Joseph's bed. "I began stroking his arm and talking to him gently," she said. "Then the doctor saw a pack of cigarettes on the TV and asked if he could take one. They were Joseph's. He wouldn't be needing them anymore, so I told him okay, I didn't think he'd mind."

"The doctor went out into the hall, smoking and pacing," Sister Loretta said. "He kept looking back in. Then he came back and sat there as I sang softly to Joseph and told him, 'Look for your parents. They're going to show you new playgrounds.' Boy, was I nervous. I'd never had a doctor watch me before. But I kept on.

"All of a sudden, Joseph smiled, tried to sit up, and held out his arms. 'Sister,' he said, 'I see them!' I asked who. 'My parents,' he told me. 'And they're just as beautiful as you said.' And right after that, he died."

Just then, the doctor's beeper went off and he started to run out of the room. Sister Loretta asked if he wanted the cigarettes, and he called back that he didn't smoke.

She sat with Joseph about ten minutes longer, still stroking him. Then she went to find the young doctor. "I wondered how he was, because he seemed so nervous. 'I know you've seen death before,'" she told him.

"'Sister,' he said, 'I've seen deaths, but only in emergency situations. It's always been so frenetic and violent. Never so peaceful like that. You know, if people have to die, everyone should be able to die like that.'"

Helping People Die Peaceful Deaths

In hospice circles, Sister Loretta—a nun of the Mother Cabrini Order and Cabrini Hospice's spiritual counselor—is known to be particularly gifted at helping people die peaceful deaths. She estimates that she's been with more than one thousand people as they have died. . . .

Sister Loretta tries to talk with each patient in his or her own symbolic or spiritual language, I found, to communicate so that anyone—no matter what his or her religious or spiritual conviction—can hear the metaphoric language of transcendence that seems to occur near death. . . .

In helping people die, Sister Loretta says that intimacy and touch are what counts, even if offering that means becoming as exposed and raw as all of us eventually become in the process of dying. In the end, love is what matters—a heart connection so real that no one feels afraid to delve into emotional business left unresolved, to share a very basic human connection of spirit, or feel alone as one dies. Sharing that experience is a need—and giving it is a skill—that the mainstream medical establishment hasn't adequately acknowledged.

Audrey Hill's Story

It is April 23, 1992. At Cabrini's inpatient unit, fifty-nine-year-old Audrey Hill is "actively dying." She has lost sixty pounds and is as thin as a starving prisoner of war. Cheeks caved in. Eyes bulging. Great gaps in her mouth where caps have fallen off her teeth. Lips pursed. When I walk into her room, she is lying in bed, clutching a soft stuffed rabbit. . . .

Audrey didn't die that April day, but in June, two months later. Her story, the story that brought her to Cabrini, illustrates what makes hospice so special, and what can make dying a time of psychological and spiritual growth in the very midst of sadness and loss.

Before she became ill, Audrey's twenty-nine-year-old son, Jonathan, later tells me, she had been "a moderate success by anyone's standards." Essentially, she was a workaholic, a career woman, raising two children, now adults, working eighteen-hour days as the founding president of a corporate travel company. Her husband had died of cancer ten years earlier. She herself was diagnosed with inoperable cervical cancer in January 1991. By February 1991 she was given only forty days to live.

Audrey's chances of survival were small, so she made the crucial decision that she'd rather have help with her pain than prolong her illness with torturous treatments. She called Cabrini Hospice nearly right away. Jonathan got a larger apartment so she could move in with him, and Cabrini sent home-care aides, nurses, a doctor, pain medications, a hospital bed. But it also sent social workers, music and art therapists, and teams of volunteers. Audrey didn't die, as doctors expected.

"She's said that except for the fact that she's dying, this has been the most terrific time of her life," Jonathan says. With her pain controlled, she was able to continue working until June 1991. After she stopped, she began cooking, doing needlepoint, learning to play the guitar from the music therapist—things she had never had time for. She also held late-night salons with her friends, having philosophical discussions on dying, reading and discussing, among other things, the books of Elisabeth Kübler-Ross. But her health steadily declined; she had a stroke, she broke her hip, she entered a roller coaster time of last breaths and revivals.

Audrey became incontinent at the beginning of April 1992, and her pain grew more severe. She'd come into the inpatient unit for a urinary catheter and a readjustment in pain medications. It seemed the end was near. On the day I met her, she'd had a serious decline. Yet something—no one could figure out what—was making her hang on.

Tying Up Loose Ends

When someone as sick as Audrey resists death, Sister Loretta later tells me, it's often because of some unfinished business. The dying person might be waiting for something—say, the birth of a grandchild or to see the wedding gown of a child about to be married, or to hear something as simple as a last "I love you" or "I forgive you" or "I'm sorry."

She views her job as helping patients by figuring out what's keeping them and helping them to resolve whatever that is, helping them to tie up, so to speak, the various strings of their lives. "Usually, if you find the right thing, people will go on the spot," she says. "You have to stay open to find out what that thing is. If you're filled with judgments, you won't find anything. But if your heart is open, you will."

By the time she died, Audrey was back home, spending

her days in a hospital bed in her son's living room. Each day, while Jonathan went to work, her twenty-six-year-old daughter, Margaret, and Margaret's two children came over. Friends came by, and in the evenings there would be the salon. Audrey lay in the center of it, beaming.

Then something began to change. She started sleeping more. When she awoke, she'd say she was getting ready to go on a journey, packing her bags, getting her ticket, things she knew she needed from the travel business. Sister Loretta encouraged Audrey's children to respond to her in the same metaphors, to speak of helping her to pack and to travel. Then Audrey said the words that revealed what had been keeping her from dying: She told everyone she was waiting for her dead husband to come and get her.

The Hospice Concept

The hospice concept rejects decisions to hasten death, but also extreme medical efforts to prolong life for the terminally ill. Rather, it aggressively treats the symptoms of disease—pain, fatigue, disorientation, depression—to ease the emotional suffering of those near death. It applies "palliative medicine," a team-based philosophy of caregiving that unites the medical know-how of doctors and nurses with the practical and emotional support of social workers, volunteer aides, and spiritual counselors. Because the goal of hospice is comfort, not cure, patients are usually treated at home, where most say they would prefer to die.

Joe Loconte, *Policy Review*, March/April 1998.

Soon, Audrey began to smile in her sleep. She held Jonathan's hand. She told Margaret and her grandchildren she loved them. She'd listen to music and talk to friends, but she was waiting. Listening. Looking at the ceiling or the wall. Then one day she announced that her husband had come, that he was here, now, in the living room with her. She grew enormously calm. She began talking to him as if he were sitting on the couch, standing near. Her four-year-old grandchild came in and pronounced the room filled with people—ghosts that no one else could see. Audrey just smiled.

A few mornings later, while Jonathan was at work and Margaret hadn't yet arrived, while Audrey and a friend were watching a movie on TV, Audrey just quietly died. The friend stood up to change the channel, and when he looked back, Audrey had gone.

Sister Loretta says that Audrey, like many dying patients, had chosen a time when it was easier to leave than if her whole family was standing by. "I feel like I'm a midwife, like I'm pushing new life," she said. "But instead of saying, 'Push, push, push,' I'm always saying, 'Go toward the light. Look for your relatives and friends.'" And that's probably just what Audrey did.

A New Approach to Dying

In America, hospice has pioneered a new approach to dying. The "hospice philosophy," as its adherents call it, focuses on this sort of psychological care, rather than solely on medical treatment. Yes, hospice practices palliative medicine, but it also attempts to help patients and families bring emotional closure to life, and to consider how a transition might best be made from this life to whatever might (or might not) lie next.

Since 1974, when hospice began in this country, it has brought Americans back to a familiarity with dying that once was there when death occurred mainly at home. With it has come a renewed intimacy with the psychological and spiritual aspects of dying and a knowledge of how to make peace both with life and with death.

The hospice philosophy has also begun feeding back into medical institutions, in the same way that the home-birthing process fed back into obstetrics two decades ago. And, as with birth, new kinds of midwives have since appeared— therapists, social workers, psychologists—who are influencing even more traditional hospital care.

The modern hospice movement began because of the zeal of an Englishwoman named Cicely Saunders, a nursing student during World War II who saw much suffering and death. She realized that what mattered most at the end of life was pain control, dignity in dying, and help addressing the psychological and spiritual pain of death itself. By the time she returned from the war, Saunders understood what she wanted to do with that knowledge.

First she got a degree in social work; next she got a degree in medicine. Then she began working in hospices around London, which at the time were places where nuns took care of the dying—rather like the refuges run by Mother Teresa in India. Dr. Saunders wanted to combine the idea of caregiving with the best of modern medicine, and particularly with the best pain medication she could find. She discovered a blend of heroin or morphine, cocaine, alcohol, and anti-nausea medication—named "the Brompton Cocktail" after the British hospital that created it—and pioneered in giving pain medication in steady doses around the clock, so pain never had a chance to peak.

In 1967, Dr. Saunders began her own hospice in a suburban section of London. She called it St. Christopher's and housed it in a sprawling old home surrounded by gardens and stone walls. It had a chapel, a child-care center, a room for afternoon tea, a bar for night discussions, and space where dying patients could spend time with their families and friends.

The Search for Meaning

The first goal for staff at St. Christopher's was to be sure patients got their pain—or other uncomfortable symptoms—under control. Then they went on to their next mission—to help the terminally ill do what Dr. Saunders considers to be their own, "real" work of dying. That, Dr. Saunders says in her lectures today, means coming to terms with "who you are, what the world is about, and what your place in it somehow is—the search for meaning." She believes a good hospice provides an environment where people can discover that wider view of life—through art, music, love, relationships, family, beauty, or religion.

During these same years, Elisabeth Kübler-Ross, M.D., a Swiss-trained physician, had begun what would become her famous Death and Dying Seminar at the University of Colorado's medical school. She would ask dying patients to come to a meeting with her medical students to describe what they were experiencing emotionally and to talk about what physicians might do to improve medical treatment and care for the dying. In essence, she asked the dying to teach her students.

Later, she brought her work to Billings Hospital, associated with the University of Chicago's medical school, and developed insights that would forever change our psychological thinking about death.

In 1969, Dr. Kübler-Ross's book *On Death and Dying* catapulted the previously taboo subject of death into modern public debate. From studying her own dying patients, she posited that from the time people receive a diagnosis of a terminal illness until they die, patients go through five emotional stages: denial, anger, bargaining, depression, and acceptance. Each stage involves specific emotional tasks. Dr. Kübler-Ross also believed that helping someone through the passage from health to illness to death is an art that can be learned. Teaching that art became her life's work.

Since Kübler-Ross's first book was published, a generation of counselors has relied on her system of stages in work with the dying, but many have misinterpreted what she wrote, expecting these stages to come in lockstep sequence. Instead, Dr. Kübler-Ross saw them as fluid, back-and-forth swings. In what order people pass through these stages, she believed, is up to them, nor do they necessarily have to go through all of them. Nor does one lead inevitably to the next.

Starting with her 1974 book, *Death: The Final Stage of Growth*, Kübler-Ross also began to suggest something more, however. What she saw earlier as five stages might be jointly called *resistance*. After that, although there may be some overlap with the last of those stages, are two additional stages in dying: a stage of life review, known as *finishing old business*, and a stage that might best be described as discovering total truth, or *transcendence*.

Finishing old business is learning to finally drop one's emotional baggage of jealousies or resentments and make an intimate, heart-to-heart connection through love. It is from this bond of openheartedness, she suggests, that transcendence, or psycho-spiritual transformation, can emerge, becoming a kind of love that is not just one-on-one, but universal, encompassing the vastness of life and humankind.

Today, many hospice workers, like Sister Loretta, have become as comfortable with such ephemeral goals in their work with the dying as they are with their basic mission to ease physical and psychological suffering.

The first hospice in America drew on the pioneering thinking of Cicely Saunders and Elisabeth Kübler-Ross through the work of Florence Wald. In the mid-1960s, Wald was dean at Yale University's school of nursing, part of the high-tech Yale–New Haven Medical Center.

Wald had watched as medicine moved from a focus on people, as she put it, to a focus on their diseases. This was of particular concern to her because of her responsibility to train future generations of nurses. It disturbed her deeply that neither death nor the impact of treatment on patients and families was even talked about. "Communication was lacking between caregivers and patients," she says, "and the way decisions were made excluded patients."

Wald sought new solutions in the work of Drs. Saunders and Kübler-Ross; she asked them both to speak at Yale. Then in 1968, she took her entire family to London and spent a month of her summer vacation at St. Christopher's nursing the dying—something she hadn't done in years.

Back in New Haven, she couldn't stop talking about this wonderful work, sharing her enthusiasm with friends and colleagues, even when she'd meet them on the street. Among those she happened to run into were two doctors and a minister who were as concerned as she was about aggressive medical treatment. They began meeting at her kitchen table in Connecticut and others soon joined them. So it was that in Branford, Connecticut, in 1974, the first American hospice was born. Wald resigned as dean of the school of nursing to focus solely on forming this hospice and, ultimately, reshaping the care of the dying.

The Connecticut Hospice began by offering home care. Eventually, Wald and her co-founders also built an inpatient residence, but as the hospice movement has grown in America, it has commonly emphasized—as Wald's hospice (and Cabrini) does—care and medical support in patients' homes rather than in residential facilities. Here, as abroad, hospice care always tries to put the focus on humane dying. The secret is assuaging pain so that the patient's real work—the psychological and spiritual work of dying—can go on.

Whereas Dr. Saunders relied heavily on the Church of England, hospice in America became infused with a larger, more diverse spirituality. Good hospices here seem to be able to assist in life closure no matter what the religion (or lack of religion) of the dying patient. Using whatever belief system the dying person might have, good hospices seem to be able to pay attention to the mind, the body, the family, and—just as significantly—to the spirit.

"[The principle of hospice] rests on a highly questionable ideology that many terminally ill patients can and do quite reasonably find unacceptable."

Hospice Care May Not Benefit the Terminally Ill

Felicia Ackerman

Felicia Ackerman is a philosophy professor at Brown University. A recipient of an O. Henry award, she has published many short stories that deal with issues in medical ethics. In the following viewpoint, Ackerman argues that hospice—a health care option emphasizing psychological, spiritual, and comfort care for the dying—is not necessarily the best choice for all terminally ill patients. The hospice emphasis on "neither hastening nor postponing" death, for example, may not be acceptable to patients who want access to experimental therapies, life-prolonging technologies, or assisted suicide. Ideally, Ackerman concludes, hospice should simply be one among several equally available health care options for the terminally ill.

As you read, consider the following questions:

1. What principles define the National Hospice Organization's "philosophy of hospice," according to Ackerman?
2. In the author's opinion, what hospice guideline appears to be a "Goldilocks Principle" for terminal illness?
3. In Ackerman's view, what kind of problem can result from the hospice emphasis on aiding family caregivers?

Excerpted from Felicia Ackerman, "Goldilocks and Mrs. Ilych: A Critical Look at the 'Philosophy of Hospice,'" *Cambridge Quarterly of Healthcare Ethics*, vol. 6, 1997. Reprinted with permission from Cambridge University Press.

Anyone who thinks contemporary American society is hopelessly contentious and lacking in shared values has probably not been paying attention to the way the popular media portray the hospice movement. Over and over, we are told such things as that "Humane care costs less than high-tech care and is what patients want and need," that hospices are "the most effective and least expensive route to a dignified death," that hospice personnel are "heroic," that their "compassion and dedication seem inexhaustible," and that "few could argue with the powerful message that it is better [for dying patients] to leave wrapped in the love of family and care givers than locked in the cold, metallic embrace of a machine."

Few do argue with this message. Even in professional circles, hospices seem largely to escape the sort of critical scrutiny that society routinely gives to business, government, and the schools. This essay aims to remedy that lack. . . .

The Philosophy of Hospice

The following principles constitute the National Hospice Organization's "Philosophy of Hospice."

1. Hospice implies acceptance of death as a natural part of the life cycle.
2. When death is inevitable, hospice will neither seek to hasten it nor to postpone it.
3. Patients, their families and loved ones are the unit of care.
4. Psychological and spiritual pain are as significant as physical pain, and addressing all three requires the skills and approach of an interdisciplinary team.
5. Pain relief and symptom control are appropriate clinical goals; the goal of all intervention is to maximize the quality of remaining life through the provision of palliative therapies.
6. Care is provided regardless of ability to pay.

I will discuss these principles in turn. . . .

Fearing Death Makes Perfect Sense

In an interview shortly before his death, the terminally ill Joseph Cardinal Bernardin said, "I don't think I could be as tranquil [about my impending death] as I am if I didn't really believe [in an afterlife]." This raises some important questions. Although serenity in the face of impending death is reasonable for those who are confident they are going on to a better place, why should we expect such serenity from terminally ill people who believe their death will be "the unequivocal and permanent end of [their] existence"? Do such expectations constitute an attempt to export religiously based attitudes—attitudes that are reasonable when grounded in religious faith in the afterlife—into a context where the religious grounding that justifies these attitudes is lacking? These questions are especially important here because, although the National Hospice Organization's promotional material mentions that patients can "share their feelings" with "their own minister, priest, or rabbi [or] a chaplain, who may be part of the hospice team," the hospice movement is not officially religious and is intended to attract and care for nonreligious as well as religious people. But when people who do and those who do not believe in the afterlife talk about death, they are talking about entirely different things. For people who value their lives and do not believe in the afterlife, doesn't fearing death make perfect sense? We would be skeptical of people who claimed to value their marriages but faced the prospect of divorce serenely or who claimed to value their religious faith but were serene about the prospect of losing it. Why, then, should people who value their lives and do not believe in the afterlife be expected to face the loss of their lives with equanimity?

One popular sort of answer is that death is natural and that "renewal requires that death precede it so that the weary may be replaced by the vigorous. This is what is meant by the cycles of nature." Such a reason for serenity about one's own impending death requires great self-abnegation on the part of the terminally ill. This can hardly be attractive to people not inclined to such a sacrificial view of their own lives. . . .

Moreover, many hospice patients are facing death at an age far earlier than could be considered "natural." All these considerations point toward the following conclusion: the idea that people should face death with serenity, rather than, for example, following Dylan Thomas's famous advice to "Rage, rage against the dying of the light" illustrates that the National Hospice Organization's "philosophy of hospice"

29

includes principles that rest on a highly questionable ideology that, while valuable for some terminally ill people, can reasonably be rejected by others. . . .

A "Goldilocks Principle"

As it stands, Principle 2 is poorly formulated. Death is inevitable for everyone. Does this mean that the National Hospice Organization's "philosophy of hospice" rejects such life-prolonging measures as insulin or blood-pressure pills for people who are not terminally ill? Obviously not; this principle is intended to apply only to the sort of patient a hospice would admit in the first place—one who is terminally ill. Even so, the principle is problematic. First, it does not indicate what counts as "postponing death" and why. Bringing food to the bedside of a bedridden patient? Feeding by hand a patient who can swallow but is too weak to lift a fork? Feeding intravenously or via a feeding tube? Elsewhere, the National Hospice Organization defines "prolongation of life" as "[u]sing artificial or other medical means to extend a patient's life beyond what would otherwise be the time of natural death," but it is still not entirely clear what this amounts to. Furthermore, the rationale for the principle is unclear. Hospice care can occur in the home (the most usual setting), or in a hospital-based unit, nursing home, or freestanding hospice facility. All these settings are generally well-equipped with air conditioning and central heating, electric lights, and windowshades. Clearly, hospice philosophy is not adverse to hastening or postponing the onset of indoor light, darkness, warmth, or coolness. Why does the National Hospice Organization regard death differently? Why does its "philosophy of hospice" include what might be called a "Goldilocks Principle" for terminal illness (death by assisted suicide is too soon, death after high-tech life-prolonging treatment is too late, "natural" death is just right), when hospices do not eschew intervention through technology or other forms of human ingenuity in other areas?

[One] possible rationale is that hospice caters to terminally ill people who want to die as soon as possible, but who have scruples, religious or otherwise, against suicide. But why do these people want to die as soon as possible? One answer might be that they have (or fear) intractable pain or a low "quality of life." These, however, are precisely the sorts of problems hospices claim to be able to alleviate. If hospices can make a terminally ill patient's life so high-quality and comfortable, why are they so adverse to prolonging it? An obvious reply is that some life-prolonging treatments are painful or otherwise unpleasant. But a nonideological organization would allow each patient to consider each possible life-prolonging medical treatment individually to decide for himself whether the possible discomfort is worth the prolonged life (and some such treatments, such as lifesaving antibiotics for pneumonia, may not be uncomfortable at all), instead of categorically refusing to provide treatment whose sole aim is life prolongation, as stated in Principle 2. This is

another example of a National Hospice Organization principle that rests on a highly questionable ideology that many terminally ill patients can and do quite reasonably find unacceptable. Claims that "humane care [rather than] high-tech care . . . is what patients want and need" beg the question and obscure the issue by setting up a false dichotomy between humane care and high-tech care, overlooking the fact that for patients who want to prolong their lives and need high-tech care in order to do so, high-tech care *is* humane care. . . .

Shortchanging the Dying

This brings us naturally to a discussion of the third principle of the National Hospice Organization's "philosophy of hospice," the principle that patients, their families, and loved ones (rather than just the patients themselves) are the unit of care. Like the preceding two principles, this is a cornerstone of the hospice approach, and also like the preceding two principles, it is open to various interpretations. First, the most innocuous: Since "home is the usual care setting for hospice patients," hospice provides support for family caregivers. While this may seem unexceptionable, even here problems can arise, as the following case illustrates.

> When Patient X was diagnosed with terminal cancer in 1988, he chose hospice care, not because he was interested in receiving counseling to help him "accept death" or in discussing his personal feelings with strangers, but because he wanted to die at home and with as little pain as possible. He and his wife were told that hospice personnel normally could come to their home between 8 A.M. and 4:30 P.M. on weekdays, but were always available for house calls in an emergency. He was also given a prescription for oral morphine and told that should be adequate for pain control. The following week, when the patient suffered agonizing pain in the middle of the night (which turned out to be the last night of his life), the hospice failed to send anyone in response to his wife's numerous distress telephone calls, telling her later that she had not seemed upset enough for it to be an emergency. As she wrote in a letter to the hospice after her husband's death, "During my husband's illness, a great deal of attention was focused on me . . . by Hospice. . . . Everyone was sympathetic, and seemed quite anxious to do things for me. . . . The trouble with all this sympathy is that, given your limited

funds (and I must assume your funds are limited, everybody's are), it was directed toward the wrong person. I was perfectly healthy. My husband, on the other hand, was terribly sick. And I would gladly have forgone every sympathetic word, every hypothetical shoulder to cry on, every kind of 'support,' if only some nurse or doctor in your organization had just come out in the middle of the night when my husband was dying and given him something for his agony."

This case illustrates the point that despite the popular contemporary tendency to regard the suffering of the terminally ill and the suffering of their loved ones as on a par, they rarely are. The terminally ill patient is generally far worse off than his healthy (or at least healthier) family. A policy that abdicates medicine's traditional responsibility of putting the patient first, and instead diverts resources of time and attention from patient to family before the patient's genuine medical needs are met, risks shortchanging the dying at their time of greatest need. In recognition of these points, Principle 3 might be called "The Mrs. Ilych Principle," after the cancer patient's widow in Tolstoy's *The Death of Ivan Ilych*, who says, "For the last three days he screamed incessantly. It was unendurable. I cannot understand how I bore it; you could hear him three rooms off. Oh, what I have suffered!" Tolstoy evidently took this to indicate monumental callousness and self-centeredness. How would the hospice movement take it? . . .

Hospice Counseling May Be Unsuitable

I now turn to Principle 4. The Patient X case suggests an objection to this principle: Is dealing with even a patient's "psychological and spiritual pain" really *just* as important as giving a dying man a shot of morphine to ease his physical agony? Since a good hospice program will presumably be able to offer services in both areas, the question may be largely theoretical. And while the practice of counseling does rest on a particular ideology—the ideology that one's "psychological pain" (i.e., unhappiness) can be alleviated by discussing the intimate details of one's life with and baring one's soul to a hired professional—this is an ideology that is common to the point of being taken for granted in much of contemporary American society. Hospice counseling, however, seems to embody more controversial expectations of patients as well. First is the above-mentioned one of "accepting death," in the sense of regarding one's own impending death serenely. As I have argued, it is inappropriate to urge this attitude on all the terminally ill. . . . [Moreover,] virtually all the hospice counseling I have heard about or read about includes a heavy dose of psychobabble (e.g., "So that loss of the ability to control your own life, your own movements, it is the strong loss of your capacity to act out your personhood, but . . . in the midst of all that, we're taking what it can give us"), which makes hospice counseling unsuitable for patients with low tolerance for such language. However, the counseling component of hospice is optional and may be bypassed by patients who choose hospice simply because they want to die as painlessly as possible and without attempts at life prolongation.

Everything I have to say that bears on the fifth principle has already been covered in my discussion of the other principles, and, of course, I have no quarrel with Principle 6.

Hospice Is Just One Option

So far, the thrust of this essay has been to examine the principles of the National Hospice Organization's "philosophy of hospice" and to argue that several depend on a highly questionable ideology that many terminally ill people can and apparently do quite reasonably find unacceptable. Thus, when its principles are fully scrutinized and understood, hospice care will be seen, not as "the most effective route to a dignified death," but as just one option for the terminally ill, whose other options should include experimental attempts at cure, high-tech life-prolongation, and perhaps even assisted suicide. This reassessment of the role of hospice care has major public policy implications. One way to see this is by considering the current debate over legalizing physician-assisted suicide for the terminally ill. Although some people object to physician-assisted suicide on religious grounds, nonreligious objections are also common, often focusing on the danger that terminally ill patients may feel pressured or may actually be pressured into "choosing" the "option" of assisted suicide in order to avoid burdening their families or society. In effect, this fear is that a Gresham's Law of treatment for the dying may come to operate as assisted suicide becomes accepted as a method of dealing with terminal illness, so that this method drives out other methods, with doctors, families, and society showing progressively less tolerance for the terminally ill who choose to linger and die "naturally."

These are legitimate concerns. What is remarkable, however, is that we have not been hearing similar fears that the option of hospice care may be leading to pressure on the terminally ill to forgo the more costly options of high-tech life-prolonging or experimental curative care. Neither the popular media nor professional medical ethicists have shown concern over the possibility that the hospice option may drive out the options of high-tech life-prolonging care and experimental curative care for the terminally ill. This lack of concern seems to stem in some cases from an inability to grasp the fact that some terminal patients want to be kept alive by machines, in other cases from a cost-conscious antipathy to high-tech life prolonging care or experimental curative care for the terminally ill, and in still other cases from the belief that there is no evidence that such pressure is widespread. But there is certainly reason to believe such pressure is occurring. And I have argued elsewhere that parsimony with respect to the terminally ill is inappropriate and inhumane in a society that spends as much as we do on such nonessentials as a bloated military and the preservation of endangered species. But I am not proposing a ban on forgoing high-tech life-prolonging or experimental curative care for the terminally ill. Such a ban would be cruel as well as impractical, denying to dying patients what some of them want. I believe the same is true of assisted suicide. The solution is not to ban the practice, but to strengthen health care options for the terminally ill, so that high-tech life-prolonging care, experimental attempts at cure, hospice care, and, if necessary, assisted suicide, are all equally available options and, at least insofar as available resources are concerned, no one has to "choose" any particular one of these alternatives by default.

"*More and more often, when there's nothing left to be done but to manage the pain, patients and their families are choosing to die at home.*"

Dying at Home Benefits the Terminally Ill

Bill Berlow

Many terminally ill people prefer to die at home rather than in a hospital or other care facility, reports Bill Berlow in the following viewpoint. Dying people often enjoy a higher quality of life in their final days if they are in familiar surroundings accompanied by family and loved ones, he points out. Although a patient's choice to die at home can place great emotional strain on his or her family, many families appreciate the opportunity to nurture their dying loved ones in their last days. Berlow is the editor of the *Tallahassee Democrat*, a Florida periodical.

As you read, consider the following questions:
1. According to Berlow, why did many terminally ill patients choose to die in hospitals in the earlier part of the twentieth century?
2. Why might some families be unable to handle caring for a terminally ill patient, according to the author?
3. How should families caring for a dying patient be supported, in Berlow's opinion?

Reprinted from Bill Berlow, "Dying at Home," *Tallahassee Democrat*, September 23, 1997. Reprinted with permission.

Travis Flesher was dying. His family knew it wouldn't be long, maybe only days, before his brief life ended.

Only six months earlier, 15-month-old Travis had been diagnosed with a brain tumor. At first, his parents were hopeful—believing early surgeries could contain or remove the cancer growing in his brain.

But when those hopes were dashed in December 1996, Kyle and Nancy Flesher brought Travis home from his high-tech hospital room in Gainesville, Florida, to be with his three brothers, his toys, his songs and the reassuring sounds and smells of their house off Buck Lake Road.

There, the Fleshers decided, their baby would die.

One day when the end appeared to be near, the pain that had been under control had Travis in its grip. The more Travis moaned, the more his mother's resolve to keep him at home wavered.

Then reason overcame emotion. Travis's father, a Tallahassee, Florida, podiatrist, realized that his son's pain could be as effectively controlled with treatment at home as in a hospital. There would be no last desperate trip to the emergency room.

A few days later, on January 21, he died peacefully.

"The only thing he could feel in a hospital was, at 8 o'clock, it was time for a blood draw," said Kyle Flesher.

Home was different.

"The only thing he could feel around us was love."

Choosing to Die at Home

For decades, with the advent of miracle drugs and even more miraculous technology, the duel with death has often kept terminally ill patients—and those keeping vigil—in hospitals, nursing homes and other care facilities. But more and more often, when there's nothing left to be done but to manage the pain, patients and their families are choosing to die at home.

"It's the last great gift that you have to give and receive," said Sally Karioth, a Florida State University nursing professor and grief counselor.

And it's a gift more families in Tallahassee are trying to give.

"I feel so good now that I did what he said he wanted," said Lucille Alexander. Her late husband, the Rev. Herbert

Alexander, died of cancer at their Woodgate home in 1994, in the constant companionship of his wife of 44 years and their four daughters.

"I'm lonesome; I miss him like the dickens," said Mrs. Alexander. "But whatever he wanted us to do, I tried to do it. So now I'm at peace."

Dying at home is hardly a new trend. In fact, it's a return to the not-so-olden days. Many homes used to be built to accommodate coffins. Death was no stranger to the home; it was often all too familiar.

When penicillin and streptomycin were developed for medical use not even 60 years ago, illnesses that routinely killed people were suddenly manageable. And as medical technology grew in sophistication, attitudes about dying shifted, as people put more faith in medicine's ability to cure.

Where families had once nursed their dying relatives in bedrooms and bath tubs, fluorescent lighted hospital rooms with beeping monitors, cold metal bedpans and IVs took their place.

When Karioth arrived in Tallahassee in 1970, for example, virtually all of her work with terminally ill people and their families was in hospitals.

But already by then, attitudes about dying were beginning to shift back. Given impetus by Elisabeth Kubler-Ross's groundbreaking 1969 book *On Death and Dying*, and a fledgling American hospice movement, people in the '70s were beginning to rethink the importance of quality with regard to life's final passage.

Now, more Americans are recognizing the limitations of medicine. The hospice movement is firmly established, and the medical establishment more accepting.

And dying at home is once again becoming commonplace. "It's just a natural thing to do," said Dr. James Mabry, medical director of Big Bend Hospice. "Turn it around: Why would you do it any other way?"

Hard Work and Rewards

To be sure, bringing a loved one home to die is not for every family. It is incredibly hard work—and a terrific emotional strain.

In June 1996, after years of battling a liver disease, Collis Hamilton, 70, learned that he had only months to live. He told his wife, Liz, he didn't want to be in the hospital any longer, and wanted to return to their Quincy home to spend his final days.

"Would it bother you if I died at home?" the retired machinist asked his wife. Liz Hamilton walked away for a moment to choke back her tears. She remembered that years earlier when her 89-year-old father was dying she had been unable to cope with the emotional strain of helping to care for him.

Watching a Parent Die

In those last weeks, we children saw our father lose all the characteristics that had made him our dad—all, that is, except his faith, which was stronger than ever. He became so weak he could not make it to the bathroom without our help. He needed to be hand-fed and turned over in bed. And in the last days, when he was unable to communicate, he needed to be given pain medication rectally. As we children assisted him, we watched as he went through episodes of pain so severe he could not think—only moan in agony. . . .

Eventually the green of summer gave way to soft autumn shades of gold and red. Brittle, brown leaves gathered in the corners of the stairs and littered the sidewalk. And the hour came when my father moved from this life to eternity. Nearly all of his family was there to witness his passing. We prayed over him and talked to him, telling him it was okay to let go. He died at 2 P.M. on the anniversary of his own father's death.

Terri Fessler Boris, *U.S. Catholic*, July 1997.

This time, though, she decided to try, despite her fears. This was her husband, the father of their four children. But she was unsure she was up to the job. "I never thought I could take care of him," she said.

But with the help of the children, grandchildren, home health care and Big Bend Hospice, she managed. Collis Hamilton died August 6, 1996, his hand in the clasp of a daughter.

Not all death is quite so neat or clean. Sometimes loved

ones must deal with blood and body fluids; sometimes nasty tempers and hallucinations try their patience.

"If you're not willing to take care of the dying person as if they were a baby," don't do it, cautioned Patsy Burgess, who helped care for her dying father earlier this year. "The sick person is not going to always be cooperative or pleasant. Don't expect there will be an outpouring of gratitude."

"Some people aren't equipped to do it," acknowledged Karioth, the grief counselor. "I say this a lot: 'I know you want to keep him at home, but this is a big deal. It takes a long time for this magnificent machine to shut down. . . . It takes energy.' I encourage people to really think about it. The trick is to not make people feel guilty when they can't do it."

But if it's possible, the rewards can be great, family members say.

"Most of them are proud of themselves when it's over with," said Mabry, an oncologist who's been practicing medicine for 22 years. "They can honestly say they helped out. They go away with a feeling that they really did what was necessary, that they shouldered a burden."

That experience, he said, often helps them cope better with grief.

Simple Conversation and Memorable Moments

Herbert Alexander had a commanding presence and was beloved by former parishioners at Bethel Baptist Church, Florida A&M University students and colleagues, and old allies in the civil-rights struggle. He loved mingling; people energized and inspired him.

When he first learned that he had colon cancer in 1992, he figured it was just one more battle to wage. But by December 1993, he knew this was a fight he couldn't win.

So he went home. He'd had enough of Room 720 at Tallahassee Memorial Regional Medical Center.

"There is some trying stuff going on," said Alesia Alexander-Greene, one of Alexander's 28-year-old twin daughters who helped take care of her father when he came home to die. "It's the atmosphere and the environment you create for your loved one that you just can't re-create in Room 720."

Many days, the family celebrated simple conversation. There were other more memorable moments, too.

Toward the end, Alexander had his daughters read aloud passages from Kahlil Gibran's *The Prophet*, a favorite book that he hadn't shared with his children as they were growing up.

He began to cry. They cried with him.

"He said, 'You know, I wish I had taught this to you all. I wish I didn't need a book for all this,'" Alexander-Greene recalled tearfully. "I said, 'God, Daddy, you lived this! This is what you do! This is what you will be remembered for!'

"I honestly think it was being at home that made that possible."

It wasn't all sweetness and light. Though the Alexanders are a close-knit family, there is still "stuff" among the sisters—emotional baggage that was laid bare amid the stress of their father's passing. But they said having the opportunity to share his final weeks with him, and each other, taught them to celebrate their differences rather than to dwell on them.

"He wanted us to know that this was what life was about, being a family," said Carucha Alexander-Bowles, 45, Alexander's oldest daughter.

That's a sentiment widely expressed among those who've helped care for a dying family member.

"I think it forces you to sometimes get rid of the pettiness, and teaches you that this is real life and you need to get rid of arguments about stupid things," said Sonja Atkins, 30. Her 82-year-old grandfather, Ben Bell, died February 2, 1997, surrounded by several generations of family that live on a five-acre spread in western Leon County.

Families Need Lots of Support

Another widely shared sentiment about dying at home: You can't do it alone. Not only is help from family members essential; so is support—tuna casseroles, baby sitting, simple words of encouragement—from friends, co-workers, church members, neighbors.

And hospice. Hospice helps with many of the details—medical, financial, emotional—that are easily forgotten or swept aside in the stress of the moment. It coordinates round-the-clock support staff to nurture the dying patient and family members.

"One of the whole points of hospice is to have as little disruption of lifestyle as possible," said Diane Tomasi, public-relations director for Big Bend Hospice. "That's the reason we're there—to help them live, not to help them die."

And that's the point of being at home with a loved one as his or her life ends.

Of her last months at home with her husband, Lucille Alexander recalled:

"It was a time I would not have gotten had he been anywhere else."

"The best things you can do are to care, to learn, and to be considerate and thoughtful. The worst thing you can do is to do nothing."

Home Caregivers' Needs Should Be Respected

Danna Syltebo

Family caregivers of a terminally ill person should have their needs attended to, maintains freelance writer Danna Syltebo in the following viewpoint. In addition to facing emotional distress, these caregivers are often overwhelmed by the daily activities of caring for a dying person and would benefit from the help of others. Syltebo, who cared for a spouse who died from Lou Gehrig's disease, suggests that concerned friends be considerate and specific when offering assistance to a caregiver. One of the most valuable things a friend can do, she points out, is to spend time visiting the dying patient so that the caregiver can get a break from the duties of tending to the patient.

As you read, consider the following questions:
1. How many years did it take for Syltebo's husband to die of Lou Gehrig's disease?
2. In the author's opinion, why should a friend avoid asking a caregiver, "How are you doing?"
3. According to Syltebo, why does one need to be sensitive about what he or she chooses to discuss in the presence of a terminally ill person?

On Sunday, March 6, 1994, at 1:00 in the afternoon, after six months of tests and worry, my husband's neurologist called him to say, "It looks like you do have ALS after all." With that fatal phone call, we had confirmation of our worst fear: my 43-year-old, handsome and athletic husband, a successful dentist and father of four, would continue to grow weaker and weaker, eventually becoming completely paralyzed, unable to walk, talk, or swallow, while his mind would remain as sharp as ever. It was likely that in the coming three to four years, he would become virtually locked in his failing body and finally die from respiratory failure as the muscles in his chest atrophied. There was no known cause for Amyotrophic Lateral Sclerosis (Lou Gehrig's Disease), no cure for the disease, and not even any useful treatment for the disease.

On Saturday, July 19, 1997, at 10:00 in the evening, my husband died from Amyotrophic Lateral Sclerosis. Between that horrible day in 1994 and the day of his death, I just tried to cope the best I could. I had no medical background or training whatsoever and no experience with taking care of anyone terminally ill. As his disease progressed, I learned a little more each day and did a little more for him each day until he was completely paralyzed and I had become his hands, his voice, his legs, his connection to the world, and his means of survival. Because it is what made Mark most comfortable and because I was physically able to handle it, I was his primary caregiver and took care of him almost entirely by myself until three months before his death. At that time, when his care became unmanageable at home, we moved him permanently to a hospice center to live.

In retrospect, there are a lot of things I wish I had done better or differently, but I just did not know any better. I had to learn by the experience, as painful as that process was. While our specific circumstances, our individual personalities, and Mark's particular disease defined our needs, I believe that much of what I learned can be applied to people who are on similar courses, whether the patient is terminally ill or not.

While I would never presume to have all the right answers for people enduring these most difficult times in their lives, I do have suggestions as to how people could have better supported me in the care of my husband for those grueling three and a half years and how they could have been a true help, rather than the unwitting burden that they often were. I would probably not have any idea, even now, as to how anyone could have helped me if it had not been that occasionally someone—whether by luck, experience, or intuition—just hit upon exactly the right thing to do or say and I found myself feeling so incredibly grateful to them. While I did not at that time feel particularly grateful to those people who did everything wrong, I can look back now and recognize that I learned as much from their mistakes as I did from the people whose actions I praised.

My suggestions are simple and common sense. They are: 1. Be considerate. 2. Offer something specific. 3. Think before you speak.

Be Considerate

First and foremost, call before coming to visit and set a specific time for your visit. Even though the patient's home may look like a hospital with all the medical equipment and supplies around, it is still a home and not a hospital with established visiting hours. Do not ask, "Is it ok if I drop by to see Mark some afternoon this week?" Say instead, "I'd like to come visit Mark for an hour at 5:30 on Tuesday. Is that time convenient?" Call again about an hour before the specified time to be sure it is still a good time for both the caregiver and patient. And, most importantly, once you set that time, show up! The patient, bed-bound or house-bound, really looks forward to those visits and the caregiver takes the time to have the patient ready for the visitor. If you do not show up, you will be missed. I can still recall, with painful clarity, my husband sitting near the front door in his wheelchair, red jacket on, his rain hat and the keys to his lift van on his lap, waiting for the friend who had promised to take him out to lunch, but who never arrived.

Be prepared that, even if you do set a specific date and time, it may be that, when you arrive, what appeared to be a convenient time no longer is. The patient may be too tired or feeling too sick to receive visitors at that time. When you arrive, let the caregiver and the patient know exactly how long you intend to stay and make sure that it is not going to be too long. Tell the patient to let you know when he is tired and needs you to leave and then, by all means, do not be offended if he has to ask you to leave. Once you set the length of your visit, stick to it. Do not assume that because the patient is still smiling and seems to be enjoying your visit that it means he wants you to stay indefinitely. He is trying to be a good host; be a good guest and get out of there while you are still in his good graces.

When you visit, do not expect the caregiver to wait on both you and the patient. Come with your own drinks and snacks in a little cooler if you are going to be staying over a meal time or even during a typical appetizer time, such as after work. The caregiver has too much to do to take care of additional people. Even if the caregiver seems willing to play hostess to you, it does not mean she is happy about it. When you see the caregiver outside of the house, try to find something to say other than, "How are you DOING?" I will tell you how she is doing: she is doing lousy. She is tired, she is overwhelmed, she is sad, she is scared, and she is guilt-ridden for hoping the nightmare will not last forever. Of course, she would never tell you that in the grocery store parking lot. She would probably say, "I'm doing okay" or "I'm hanging in there" when that is not how she is feeling at all. She is trying to say what she thinks you want to hear. How about greeting her instead with, "It's nice to see you out and about. I'd like to come over and see Mark on Friday and bring him some lunch. Would that work for you?" Or, as was once wonderfully offered to me, "How nice to see you! Do you have a few minutes right now so that I can buy you a cup of coffee?" Believe me, you will make her day with either of those offers. . . .

Offer Something Specific

Try to avoid asking, "What can I do for you?" or saying, "If there is ever anything I can do for you, please don't hesitate to ask" or any variation of this theme. Those offers are too vague to be helpful. The caregiver is exhausted and stressed, just trying to get through the days. She does not want to have to come up with ideas for other people so that they can feel helpful. If you have no intention of really helping, do not offer. If you sincerely want to help, then you come up with the ways to do that; do not expect the caregiver to do it for you. Offer something specific. Say, "I'd like to come over on Friday at noon with lunch for Mark. I have two full hours free, so you can get out of the house while I'm visiting with him." Be sure before you offer to bring a meal for the patient that you are aware of any special dietary restrictions. In Mark's case, as his swallowing became impaired, certain foods became dangerous to eat and I often had to stop people at the door who were bringing him cookies or nuts after he had lost the ability to safely eat them.

Providing Emotional Support

Being excluded from the lives of others is very painful to a dying person. Conversations and activities with family members help dying loved ones feel that they are a part of family life. The presence of children can be comforting and the physical touch of loved ones can be reassuring.

The location of the dying person's bed also can be important. Keeping the bed near family activities helps to increase social interaction and may improve the dying person's emotional well-being. Hospice professionals and others with experience in caring for the dying can help enhance communication among the dying person and family members.

Choice in Dying, Informational Pamphlet, 1996.

Another way to help is to prepare a full dinner for the entire family—not just the entree, but all the side dishes as well—and call to say you will be dropping it by that afternoon. It is best if it is a meal which could either be prepared that night or put in the freezer for future use. Do not put it in a dish that you need back right away and do not expect the caregiver to keep track of your baking dishes or salad bowls and return them to you. Disposable baking dishes (the foil kind) and zip-lock plastic bags for salads and rolls are the best to use, but if you use something other than disposable containers, call the caregiver and set a definite time to come and retrieve them from her and suggest to her that she just leave them on the front porch on a specific day so that it does not have to be a convenient visiting time as well. A caregiver does not want to have your dishes on the counter as a reminder that they belong to someone else and she usually cannot make a special trip to return them to you.

Still another way to help would be to organize a work party to clean the caregiver's house, clean the gutters, take junk to the dump, or weed the yard and mow the lawn. By all means, check with the caregiver as to what work you are planning to do and for a convenient time to do that work. When you are on your way over for a scheduled visit and you are calling to check that the time is still convenient, offer to pick up any supplies or groceries that might be needed. . . .

As a former caregiver, I could make lists of chores which would have been nice to hand over to friends and family members who were begging to help. But, the reality is, that completing those little tasks was never really the problem for me. The top item on any list I would create would be this: Sit with my husband so that I can get a break.

Even our health insurance company recognized that the primary need of a home caregiver was getting a break, or what they term "respite care". The policy did not pay for nursing or aide care in our home for my husband. It did not pay for the care my husband received while living in the hospice center. Instead, it paid only for "respite care", time when a professional person would come in and take care of my husband for the sole purpose of giving me a break from that duty. They even dictated how that time could be used, requiring that the aides be scheduled in no shorter than four hour increments. Anything less than that was not considered true respite care. . . .

Think Before You Speak

Be sensitive in your choice of topics for conversation. If you are not a member of the immediate family or have not been part of the patient's life on a frequent and regular basis before and during his illness, accept that you do not know everything that has gone on or why the patient is being cared for in the way he is, but that there are good, sound reasons for all the choices made. Realize that no major choices would be made without consulting the patient nor without looking at all the feasible alternatives, particularly when the patient is fully alert mentally, as my husband was.

Do not open up subjects that are potentially painful or controversial without checking with the caregiver first. People were not helpful when they went to the hospice center to visit Mark and asked him things such as, "Why are you here instead of at home?" or "Are you happier here?" or even, "Are they treating you well here?" If the family has chosen this option, you can assume that the care is good and that a lot of time, emotion, and thought went into the decision.

One of the best examples of what not to say happened about a month after my husband had been moved to the hospice center. A former dental patient of my husband's, whom I had never met and who had not visited him since his disability retirement, walked into his room unannounced and started in on a long speech about how she had taken care of her mother at home until the day she died. She kept saying over and over, "It is certainly do-able to take care of someone at home." Four weeks of work by the family to assure Mark that the hospice center was the absolute best care available for him went out the window in that one afternoon. She did not take the time to confer with me before talking with Mark. She did not know that his disease had reached a point which required three people round the clock to move him, bathe him, medicate him, and dress him and that hiring a team that size for home would be financially and logistically impractical if not impossible. She spoke before she thought. That woman walked away, never came to see him again, and never knew the destructive nature of her words. For two weeks after her visit, he wrenched my heart as he begged me daily to take him home and then got angry with me when I reiterated all the reasons why he had to remain where he was. . . .

Do not expect the caregiver to explain the patient's disease to you. Over and over, people expected me to explain the physiological differences between Multiple Sclerosis, which my husband did not have and I knew almost nothing about, and Amyotrophic Lateral Sclerosis, which, having been educated in English Literature and Accounting, I did not have the medical background to sufficiently explain. You have as much capacity—and certainly more time—to do the research on the disease as the caregiver has. She should not have to give you the painful details of what the disease is doing to the patient, what his current symptoms are, or what his prognosis is. If she offers that information, fine, but do not continually ask, "How is he?" or "How much longer does he have?" Mark was never "fine" and in fact was always worse, but I often answered that way to appease the asker, and I never really knew how much longer he would live until we were within hours of the end. Instead of asking those questions, just be there for both the patient and the caregiver as often as you feel comfortable and do not worry about how much time he has left. Unless you are leaving on an extended vacation, it does not really matter, does it?

Pick up a book on the disease so you know exactly what both the caregiver and the patient are dealing with. Get on the internet and find out all the current information about studies being done, support groups available, and service groups available. But realize that the caregiver does not have free time to read all the books you have read, so do not bring them by the house for her. If there is pertinent information that you feel would really benefit her or the patient, then paraphrase it and share it or leave her the internet address where she can seek out information for herself. Do not just leave a book; it will not get read and she does not want to worry about which books have to be returned to which people. . . .

The Value of Spending Time with the Sick

All of our lives, at one time or another, will be touched by a friend or family member who is critically or terminally ill. Perhaps we will be the patient ourselves, perhaps we will be the primary caregiver, or perhaps we will be on the outside, trying desperately to help, but not knowing what to say or what to do. I understood that, as Mark's wife and his primary caregiver, no one else could really share the weight of his care with me. It was my duty to see that he always got the very best care, whatever I had to sacrifice to ensure that. As an outsider, there is only so much that you really can do to help, but you can certainly avoid making the burden greater than it already is and you can probably give occasional breaks to the caregiver to allow her to recharge her energy. Accomplishing just that much helps more than you can imagine.

As a caregiver, I could easily forgive the people who did not know what to say and often said the wrong things to me or to my husband. What I found more difficult to forgive was the unwillingness of friends and family to just spend time with him. Even if they could come up with no way of helping me, the least they could have done was to come see him and let him know that he was loved.

Sadly, and much too often, people waited until he was beyond the point of being able to interact with them before they came to see him. They came only to say their final farewells to him and assuage their own guilt, rather than coming to see him throughout the illness in order to help him get through it. The visits were terribly frustrating for Mark because he could not speak to his guests and he was embarrassed to be seen by people who had not watched his slow decline. He turned down most visitors, in fact, as he reached the end, because it was such a struggle for him to communicate. The only people he always wanted to see were the ones who had been coming on a regular basis and understood his limitations. If you were not one of those people who had an ongoing relationship with the patient throughout his illness, perhaps it would be better that you stay away at the end. Accept that you were not strong enough to be a good friend or relative during the time that your visits could have helped and make a vow that you will do better the next time you are faced with this situation.

The best things you can do are to care, to learn, and to be considerate and thoughtful. The worst thing you can do is to do nothing.

"Studies show that a majority of dying patients experience severe, undertreated pain."

Patients Should Be Given Better Treatments for Pain

Part I: Ellen Goodman; Part II: Warren E. Leary

The authors of the following two-part viewpoint contend that the problem of undertreated pain among the terminally ill must be addressed. In Part I, syndicated columnist Ellen Goodman argues that severe pain often causes the fatally ill to lose their will to live; compassion demands that these patients be given adequate medication to prevent needless suffering during the dying process. In Part II, *New York Times* writer Warren E. Leary reports that recent improvements in medicine have resulted in life-sustaining technologies that only prolong the dying process and do not effectively control pain. The medical community needs to focus on relieving suffering and improving end-of-life care, Leary maintains.

As you read, consider the following questions:

1. According to Goodman, why was Dr. Paul Bilder reprimanded by the Oregon state board of medical examiners?
2. Where do the majority of deaths occur, according to Leary?
3. According to Dr. Christine Cassel, cited by Leary, why do doctors underuse pain medications?

Part I: Reprinted from Ellen Goodman, "A Right to Pain Management," *The Boston Globe*, September 27, 1999. Reprinted with permission from the Washington Post Writers Group. Part II: Reprinted from Warren E. Leary, "Many in U.S. Denied Dignified Death," *The New York Times*, June 5, 1997. Reprinted with permission.

I

D r. Paul Bilder may never become a famous name in the history of end-of-life care at the end of the millennium.

Bilder is no Jack Kevorkian, the pathologist who brazenly defied the law and forced the country to deal with assisted suicide. Nor is he Timothy Quill, the internist whose published admission that he helped a terminal patient to die encouraged other doctors out of the closet.

But Dr. Bilder represents a landmark nevertheless. In September 1999, the Oregon pulmonary specialist became the first doctor in the country to be disciplined by a state board of medical examiners for *under*treating pain in his patients.

The patients in his "care" were not all dying, but some experienced the kind of suffering that could have been alleviated—and wasn't. Once, Bilder prescribed only Tylenol for a terminally ill man with cancer. Another time, he gave a patient only a fraction of the drug that the patient needed and the hospice nurse suggested. He refused morphine or similar pain medication for an 82-year-old with congestive heart failure.

After being challenged on this mistreatment, Dr. Bilder signed an order admitting that he showed unprofessional or dishonorable conduct and negligence. For pain treatment and his skills at talking with patients.

It's not a surprise that the first such case in which a doctor is taken to task for undermedicating pain and suffering happened in Oregon. The state was after all, also the first in the country to pass a law legalizing doctor-assisted suicide.

A Long-Delayed Discussion

Even those who deeply oppose such legislation acknowledge the good news about the ethical wrangling over the end of life. We have finally embarked on a long delayed discussion about the need for palliative care, for compassionate treatment, for understanding the real experience of illness.

Indeed in the same week that Dr. Bilder was disciplined for failing his patients, the British medical journal *Lancet* published a Canadian study showing that, even among terminal cancer patients, the will to live fluctuates a great deal. In the course of just one day, attitudes toward living and dying change. This research shows what common sense suggests: Physical pain affects attitudes about living and dying.

Yet even in Oregon, as a recent study from the Center for Ethics in Healthcare showed, a third of people in the last week of life suffer moderate to severe pain. If pain is behind despair, if pain is the primary rationale for supporters of doctor-assisted suicide, how much of the ethical debate is really a medication debate?

The irony is that this controversy about pain and medicine has also gone on and on. Twenty years ago doctors were penalized for giving too much medication—specifically narcotics.

In the early 1980s a pain specialist was accused of overprescribing by the California medical board. In February 1999 another California doctor was charged with murder. The prosecutor said that he was really supplying drugs to users.

For a long time, our paranoia about drugs and addiction, especially narcotics, has affected the fear and freedom that doctors have to ease pain. We have acted as if a terminally ill 80-year-old patient were a junkie about to rise from her death bed and rob a grocery store. We still deny marijuana for AIDS and chemo patients. We deny heroin to the dying.

The War on Drugs has done its collateral damage on sick civilians. But now in Oregon a doctor is also disciplined for prescribing Tylenol when the patient needed morphine.

This is not just damned if you do and damned if you don't. We are again in a time of change.

A Right to Pain Management

The health community is gradually adopting standards that recognize a right to pain management. Nineteen states now have laws that protect doctors from prosecution for prescribing painkillers as long as they are used to kill pain. And Oregon has, at last, stated that good care means reducing suffering.

In the end, the most important part of Dr. Bilder's "punishment" requires him to learn how to listen to patients. In the midst of an ongoing national debate about a doctor's role in providing a compassionate death, what he'll hear is the desire for just plain compassion.

II

Too many Americans are denied a chance to die well because of inadequate care and lack of understanding of their needs, an expert panel from the Institute of Medicine said in June 1997.

The 12-member panel said many Americans suffered preventable pain and stress at the end of life. The experience is so poorly managed by doctors and other health workers, as well as insurers, that many people see death as a degrading, painful episode that leads to talk of assisted suicide, the panelists said.

"Americans have come to fear that they will die alone, and that they will die in distress or pain," Dr. Christine Cassel, chairwoman of the panel, said at a news conference. "This does not have to be the case."

There are signs that the health care system is finally taking the issues of dying seriously, but too many are still dying without the benefit of skillful and compassionate care, said Dr. Cassel, chairwoman of geriatrics and adult development at Mount Sinai Medical Center in New York City.

Ill-Prepared to Deal with Death

American medicine emphasizes high-tech cures, surgery and aggressive treatment to save patients, the committee said in a report, and not what happens when death becomes inevitable. Many doctors are ill-prepared to deal with death or to help patients and their families face the end of life, it said.

Studies show that a majority of dying patients experience severe, undertreated pain and many feel that modern treatment often helps prolong agony while failing to prepare patients adequately for death, committee members said.

"It is perverse that fears of both overtreatment and abandonment have driven the current debate over physician-assisted suicide," Dr. Cassel said. The debate over assisted suicide, on which the committee did not take a position, is a sad commentary on the state of dying, she said.

"No one should view suicide as their best option because they lack effective and compassionate care as they die," she said.

The report called for better training of health-care professionals, changes in Federal and state laws that inhibit the use of pain-relieving drugs, research on how people view and adjust to dying, and testing new insurance and other payment options for chronic, not just acute, illness.

The study, which was sponsored primarily by contributions from private health foundations, noted that more than 70 percent of the two million Americans expected to die in 1997 will be over age 65 and that this percentage would rise as the population aged.

"Before we try assisted suicide, Mrs. Rose, let's give the aspirin a chance."

J.B. Handelsman. Reprinted by permission of The Cartoon Bank, a division of the *New Yorker* magazine.

With the reduction of death from communicable diseases and dramatic increases in average life span, death from most of the nation's leading killers—such as heart disease, cancer and AIDS—often follow a period of serious, chronic illness, the committee said. Because of this, it said, three-quarters of all deaths occur in hospitals and nursing homes, and less than 20 percent of people die at home.

After years of discussions about inadequately treating pain in people with life-threatening illnesses, problems persist, the report said. Changes are needed in flawed drug prescription laws that control the distribution of narcotics and other potent pain relievers, burdensome regulations and state policies that impede effective use of drugs, it said.

"We still have a real problem in this country with untreated pain," Dr. Cassel said. Concerns about drug use, including unreasonable fears of addiction, create a climate in which doctors underuse pain medications, she said.

Robert Burt, a professor at Yale Law School and a member of the committee, said legitimate concerns about trafficking in narcotics had become a barrier to treatment. "There is a tension between the need to control illegal drugs and the need for palliative care to control pain," he said. "Controls are much more rigid than they need to be."

The Culture of Medicine

Dr. Cassel said the culture of medicine needed to be changed to deal with death realistically. Too often, she said, death is viewed as a failure of medicine. "No one is told they did a good job with a patient who died," she said.

Medical school training focuses on acute illness and heroic cures, and there is little attention to assessing and managing pain, or in helping patients prepare for death, she said. "Caring for a patient who is dying is one of the greatest privileges of being a doctor," she said.

Dr. George Thibault, chief medical officer at Brigham and Women's Hospital in Boston, said pain was only one symptom afflicting the dying that is receiving inadequate attention. Terminal patients also suffer with breathing difficulties, nausea, vomiting, fatigue, malaise, confusion, nightmares and sleep disorders, and other problems that are often not well understood or controlled, said the committee member.

Good Dying

Another panelist, Dr. Joanne Lynne, director of George Washington University's Center to Improve the Care of the Dying, said people need to understand that they could have a good death, using the extra time to prepare and put their lives in order. "We have to start telling each other stories about good dying," Dr. Lynne said.

The Institute of Medicine, an affiliate of the National Academy of Sciences, undertook the study after determining that many issues concerning dying patients were not being addressed adequately.

"There remains a serious gap between the choices people want at the end of their lives and what they are now permitted."

Patients Should Be Given More Control over Their Deaths

Faye Girsh

Faye Girsh is executive director of the Hemlock Society USA, a right-to-die organization headquartered in Denver, Colorado. In the following viewpoint, Girsh argues that the terminally ill should have more medical choices at the end of their lives. While dying patients are allowed to refuse life-prolonging treatments or to choose hospice care, Oregon is thus far the only state in the United States that permits physician-assisted suicide. Girsh contends that fatally ill patients should be able to consider all possible alternatives, including physician aid in dying, as death approaches.

As you read, consider the following questions:
1. What Supreme Court case established the right to refuse unwanted medical treatment?
2. What criteria must be met before patients are allowed aid in dying under Oregon's Death with Dignity Act?
3. According to Girsh, what percentage of surveyed Americans believe that the terminally ill should have a right to doctor-assisted suicide?

Reprinted from Faye Girsh, "Death with Dignity: Choices and Challenges," *USA Today*, March 2000. Copyright ©2000 the Society for the Advancement of Education. Reprinted with permission.

While Americans consider themselves free to live the lives they choose, most don't realize that this freedom ends when it comes to selecting a peaceful death over a life filled with unbearable pain and suffering. Euthanasia advocate Jack Kevorkian's conviction of second-degree murder for assisting in the nationally televised suicide of terminally ill Thomas Youk has shown that, despite achieving great legal successes over the last 25 years, Americans have a long way to go in securing the freedom to die with dignity when confronted by terminal illness.

Interest in the right-to-die issue has become increasingly important as people are now enjoying longer, healthier lives than at any time in history. Diseases that kill suddenly and prematurely have been virtually wiped out in developed countries. What are left are conditions that often result in lingering, agonizing declines—cancer, stroke, Parkinson's disease, and amyotrophic lateral sclerosis (Lou Gehrig's disease), to name a few. Ninety percent of the people who die each year are victims of prolonged illnesses or have experienced a predictable and steady decline due to heart disease, diabetes, or Alzheimer's disease.

The Need for End-of-Life Options

Medicine can keep people alive with artificial organs, transplants, and machines—even artificial food and water—rather than allowing a terminally ill patient a quick death through pneumonia or organ failure. Modern medicine often does more than prolong living—it actually extends dying.

A study of dying patients in five major medical centers revealed that 59% would have preferred to receive just care to make them more comfortable, instead of the aggressive treatment they got. Another study surveyed Canadian patients who identified five areas of importance at the end of life: receiving adequate pain and symptom management; avoiding prolonged dying; achieving a sense of control; relieving the burden on loved ones; and strengthening relationships with people.

A big advancement in caring for terminally ill patients has come with the growth in hospice care, which started with one facility in 1974 and has grown to almost 3,000 nationwide, making it accessible to most Americans. Hospice care is designed to control pain and provide physical and spiritual comfort to those who are dying. It neither prolongs nor hastens death. While hospices have dramatically improved end-of-life care, there remains a serious gap between the choices people want at the end of their lives and what they are now permitted.

Patients' rights at the end of their lives take two forms— the right to refuse medical treatment when faced with inevitable death and the right to secure a doctor's help in ending suffering at the end of life. It took the deaths of two young women—Karen Ann Quinlan and Nancy Cruzan—to give every American the right to make medical decisions in advance. Both had gone into irreversible comas following accidents and, after lengthy legal battles, their parents received permission from the courts to disconnect their daughters' life support.

In Cruzan's case, which took place 14 years after Quinlan's, the Supreme Court ruled that every American has the right to refuse unwanted medical treatment for any reason, even if it leads to death. This includes the right to refuse food and fluids. Justice William Brennan wrote, "Dying is personal. And it is profound. For many, the thought of an ignoble end, steeped in decay, is abhorrent. A quiet, proud death, bodily integrity intact, is a matter of extreme consequence."

Oregon's Death with Dignity Act

Physician-assisted dying is legal today only in Oregon, where voters legalized the practice in 1994 and again in 1997. During the first year, 23 patients obtained medication from their doctors, but just 15 used it to end their lives. Six others died natural deaths, and two were still living when the study was completed. This shows that people want to know they have a choice, but not all will take advantage of it. Under the provisions of the Oregon Death with Dignity Act:

• The request must come voluntarily from a mentally competent, terminally ill, adult resident of Oregon.

• Two physicians must examine the patient to confirm the diagnosis and prognosis.

• A mental health professional must be consulted if either

doctor has a question about mental competence, depression, or coercion.

• All other alternatives must be presented and explained to the patient.

• The patient must make witnessed requests orally and in writing.

• After a 15-day waiting period, the patient receives a physician's prescription for a lethal dose of medication, which can be filled following a two-day waiting period.

• All prescriptions under the Death with Dignity law must be reported to the state health department.

• The patient is then free to take the medication when and if he or she wishes. Family, friends, and a doctor may be present.

Thanks to the laws allowing patients to refuse medical treatment and the growing availability of hospice care, we have more control over how we die. The changes happened because people demanded better care and more options at the end of life. These progressive measures were opposed at first because of the fear of abuse. Naysayers predicted that giving individuals the choice to live or die would lead to a cheapening of human life. Now, though, they don't have to have treatment they don't want and can rely on someone they select to speak for them when they can't. They can refuse additional treatment, opt for hospice care, and hasten their death by refusing food and water. These choices work to give the terminally ill more control, but they still haven't gone far enough.

Doctor-Assisted Deaths

In a survey of 30,000 Americans over the age of 55, 65% said that people with a terminal illness should have a legal right to hasten their death with a doctor's assistance. Carol Poenisch, the adult daughter of a woman with Lou Gehrig's disease who ended her life with the help of Kevorkian, described her mother's condition in the *New England Journal of Medicine*. Her mother could not speak, support her head, or swallow. Extreme weakness meant she required help to do everything. When she discovered that Kevorkian could help her die, she made that choice. According to her daughter, "She was much more at ease with her illness and her death than I. She was much braver about it, and she was calm." Her mother's decision was not unusual for people suffering from this debilitating disorder—56% of patients with Lou Gehrig's disease say they would consider making the same choice.

Rational Requests for Suicide

In my view, the most compelling reason to favor rational suicide is that there are persons with intractable suffering for whom there are no satisfactory options, and these individuals can make a rational choice to hasten death. The person who is suffering is the only one who can define the suffering and make a determination about its bearability and acceptability. A rational request for suicide must be responded to in a timely, humane, comprehensive, and holistic manner.

Margaret L. Campbell, *Contemporary Perspectives on Rational Suicide*, ed. James L. Werth Jr., 1999.

After three operations for lung cancer, a 62-year-old woman could hardly breathe and suffered suffocating chest pain. Although hospice care helped with her symptoms, she was ready to die. She contacted the Hemlock Society, which provides information and support for a peaceful death. Through the Caring Friends program, a trained volunteer worked with her and her husband to ensure that she had exhausted all the alternatives, that she knew the right way to end her life, and that a medical professional was in attendance when she died. The woman found a compassionate physician who, risking his license and liberty, supplied her with the right amount of lethal medication. She died peacefully, in the company of her husband, best friend, and a Caring Friends volunteer. Because this woman lived in a state where assisting a death is illegal, everyone involved, including the Hemlock Society, could have been subject to prosecution.

Why is it necessary to involve doctors? Why can't people just kill themselves? In this country, suicide is not a crime. However, suicide, as it traditionally is thought of, involves violence, uncertainty, and pain for the family. Some terminally ill people end their lives while they can, often prematurely, fearing there will be no way to do it if they wait too long. Without the reassurance that someone would be there to help, people often commit suicide violently and use the wrong methods, which can traumatize their loved ones in the process.

Austin Bastable, a Canadian man with multiple sclerosis, who died with the help of Kevorkian, said, "Knowing that such dedicated people exist, I could afford to live longer than I originally had planned—because I knew that I no longer had to rely solely upon my limited abilities to end my life." Those with terminal illnesses should be able to die peacefully, gently, quickly, and with certainty—in the arms of people they love. This requires medical assistance.

A Typical Case

Let's consider a typical case, that of Rose, an 82-year-old woman with terminal pancreatic cancer. She has made peace with her dying and receives care at home from a hospice nurse. She is on a morphine pump to control her pain, although she dislikes being sedated. Weak, tired, and nauseated, she knows the end is near and begs for a quick, peaceful death. Her children want to help her, but, because aiding her to die is against the law, they can only watch while she suffers.

Many people, like Rose's children, have cared for a loved one who wants to die, but cannot get the assistance to make it happen. Asking someone for help to die, or being asked to help, is not only emotionally difficult, it could lead to breaking the law.

This tortuous situation occurs every day. If she were hooked up to some kind of treatment, Rose could legally and easily request that it be stopped and she could die, but she isn't. So her children must stand by when their mother is begging them to help her die, and they have to continue to watch her suffer.

Except in Oregon, the law does not allow the family to work with a terminally ill patient's doctor to help end his or her suffering. Some physicians in other states break the law and provide assistance; some family members try to help, but don't know how, and the attempt fails tragically. The patient and the family should be able to discuss their end-of-life choices with their doctor and explore all other alternatives, but be able to know there will be aid in dying if the situation is hopeless and the request persistent.

Know Your Rights

Each of us needs to make plans to ensure that the end of life remains in our control. Just as we write wills to dispose of our worldly goods, we can make decisions about what medical treatment is acceptable and what is not. You can write a living will, which says you do not want drastic measures taken if you have no hope for recovery. You can choose a person to make your health care decisions if you are unable to. (This is called the Durable Power of Attorney for Health Care or Health Care Proxy.) That individual should be someone you trust, who knows what you want, and will fight for your rights.

If you agree that physician aid in dying should also be a choice for terminally ill, mentally competent adults who request it, there are things you can do:

- Join an advocacy organization, such as the Hemlock Society, that supports legal change.
- Tell your state and national representatives how you feel.
- Vote if there is an initiative in your state.
- Discuss the issue with your family, doctor, and spiritual advisor.

How you die should be your choice. As poet Archibald MacLeish said, "Freedom is the right to choose: the right to create for yourself the alternative of choice. Without the possibility of choice and the exercise of choice, a man is not a man but a member, an instrument, a thing."

Periodical Bibliography

The following articles have been selected to supplement the diverse views presented in this chapter. Addresses are provided for periodicals not indexed in the *Readers' Guide to Periodical Literature*, the *Alternative Press Index*, the *Social Sciences Index*, or the *Index to Legal Periodicals and Books*.

Richard Burnham	"Hospice Care: Making an Informed Choice," *USA Today Magazine*, March 1999.
Ira Byock	"Why Do We Make Dying So Miserable?" *Washington Post*, January 22, 1997. Available from 1150 15th St. NW, Washington, DC 20071.
Joseph A. Califano Jr.	"Physician-Assisted Living," *America*, November 14, 1998.
Denise Carlson	"Walking with a Dying Friend," *Moody*, May/June 1998. Available from the Moody Bible Institute, 820 N. LaSalle Blvd., Chicago, IL 60610.
John F. Kavanaugh	"The Shame of Our Dear Humanness," *America*, December 19–26, 1998.
Maria L. LaGanga	"Trying to Figure the Beginning of the End," *Los Angeles Times*, October 15, 1999. Available from Reprints, Times Mirror Square, Los Angeles, CA 90053.
Joe Loconte	"Hospice, Not Hemlock," *Policy Review*, March/April 1998.
Steven A. Schroeder	"Dying Patients and Their Families," *Vital Speeches of the Day*, March 1, 2000.
Pam Sebastian	"Making Friends for Life," *Wall Street Journal*, December 11, 1996.
Sheryl Gay Stolberg	"As Life Ebbs, So Does Time to Elect Comforts of Hospice," *New York Times*, March 4, 1998.
Marilyn Webb	"At the End of Life, a Blind Bureaucracy," *New York Times*, March 11, 1998.
Richard L. Worsnop	"Caring for the Dying," *CQ Researcher*, September 5, 1997. Available from 1414 22nd St. NW, Washington, DC 20037.

How Should the Physical and Emotional Pain of Terminal Illness Be Addressed?

Chapter Preface

Many of the world's religious traditions offer guidance to terminally ill people and their caregivers. Christians may reflect on the significance of the crucified Christ to gain insight during the dying process; Jews often recite prayerful chants and concentrate on the *nefresh*, or soul, of a dying individual; Buddhists may perform *Phowa*—visualization of the divine presence filling up and transforming the dying person's being. But in modern America's largely secular society, many maintain, such spiritual and philosophical support for the dying is sadly lacking.

The reason for this, according to doctor and ethicist Laurence O'Connell, is partly because "health care and spirituality have come to be seen as largely separate domains in many Western countries." Indeed, most medical personnel in the United States rely on biological explanations for disease and technical approaches to therapy. Though they may be prepared to address the scientific aspects of terminal illness, clinicians are often at a loss when faced with the distress of a dying patient who asks, "why me?" As O'Connell points out, "A dying person's questions concerning the meaning and purpose of one's life, the meaning of pain and suffering, confront health care providers . . . with a dilemma: What role should they play in eliciting and attempting to meet the spiritual needs of their patients?" Even patients who have no religious leanings often yearn to assess the significance of their lives, contends O'Connell.

While counselors and chaplains do address some of these needs, some in the medical community contend that health care providers themselves should become more informed about the metaphysical aspects of dying. As a result, a growing number of medical schools and health care institutions are making efforts to train clinicians about the spiritual and psychological quandaries associated with the dying process.

A fatal diagnosis is one of the most painfully devastating crises that people may encounter. The authors of the following chapter offer several insights on how the physical and emotional pain of terminal illness should be addressed.

*"Policies to ensure adequate treatment
of symptoms should take precedence
over legalization of physician-assisted
suicide and euthanasia."*

The Medical Community Should Emphasize Pain Treatment over Euthanasia

American Pain Society

The American Pain Society (APS) is the U.S. chapter of the International Association for the Study of Pain, a group of clinical researchers investigating the treatment of pain caused by human diseases. The following viewpoint is an APS position statement outlining the organization's stance on symptom relief for terminally ill patients. The APS contends that the medical community must become more aggressive in treating the pain associated with fatal illnesses, particularly since severe pain can cause patients to long for death. Effective pain treatment should be emphasized over assisted suicide, the APS maintains; moreover, laws must protect health professionals whose use of painkilling drugs unintentionally hastens a patient's death.

As you read, consider the following questions:
1. According to the APS, why are the painful symptoms of terminal illness often undertreated in America's health care system?
2. Why are physicians often reluctant to administer strong analgesics to dying patients, according to the authors?
3. In the opinion of the APS, which symptoms of advanced illness have not been well researched?

Reprinted from American Pain Society, "Treatment of Pain at the End of Life," 2000. Reprinted with permission.

APS Task Force on Pain, Symptoms, and End of Life Care: Mitchell Max, MD, Chair; James Cleary, MD; Betty Ferrell, PhD FAAN; Kathleen Foley, MD; Richard Payne, MD; Barbara Shapiro, MD.

The American Pain Society is the U.S. chapter of the International Association for the Study of Pain. Its 3,000 members include many of the leading basic and clinical researchers in the epidemiology, mechanisms, and treatment of acute and chronic pain caused by the range of human diseases. The following position statement has been prepared by the society's Task Force on Pain, Symptoms, and End of Life Care and has been approved by the board of directors.

1. We recognize that the current debate over physician-assisted suicide and euthanasia reflects a broad public concern that terminal illness is often accompanied by severe pain and other symptoms that make death seem preferable.

2. Pain and other symptoms at the end of life can usually be relieved if clinicians have the training and resources to focus on this goal, but current treatment often falls short. Well-trained clinicians can provide adequate pain relief for more than 90% of dying cancer patients. Patients can be reassured that in the occasional case where the best treatments cannot allow the patient to be alert and relatively comfortable, intravenous sedatives can relieve all symptoms in the last days of life. However, a substantial proportion of patients, particularly those in minority groups, receive inadequate analgesic treatment (Cleeland et al., 1994). Suicidal wishes in patients with advanced disease are closely linked to unrelieved pain and to mood alterations such as depression and anxiety, which like pain, frequently respond to clinician treatment if the clinician identifies and addresses them (Foley, 1995).

3. Despite the best intentions of clinicians, pain and symptom control is often suboptimal because the entire healthcare system has been designed around cure of disease rather than palliation (Max, 1990). There have been many demonstrations of major improvements in pain treatment within a healthcare organization, but programs that do this must redesign many aspects of the way care is delivered (Jacox et al., 1994; American Pain Society Quality of Care

Committee, 1995). Essential ingredients in such programs include the following:

- Physicians, nurses, patients, and families must be educated about pain treatment, and materials to guide treatment must be readily available to assist clinicians in writing orders.

- The organization and all of its professionals must make themselves accountable to all of their patients—ranging from newborns to the elderly—for attentive treatment of pain.

- Pain must be made "visible" in the organization—routinely charted as a "fifth vital sign" so that unrelieved pain triggers a prompt response.

- Quality improvement activities may be used to encourage steady improvement in the treatment of pain in the organization.

- Expert consultants and "high technology" pain treatment interventions such as patient-controlled analgesia and epidural catheters must be available (either within the healthcare organization or by referral) for the minority of cases in which simpler measures do not suffice.

- Policies on reimbursement for health professionals, medications, and other palliative treatments (e.g., counseling, cognitive treatment for symptoms, and other supportive care), and controlled substance regulations must be designed so that they do not create barriers to symptom treatment.

- Patients' and families' values and preferences regarding end-of-life care must be respected.

4. Policies to ensure adequate treatment of symptoms should take precedence over legalization of physician-assisted suicide and euthanasia. This position statement seeks to improve symptom relief for all dying patients within the next 5–10 years, not just for the few patients who may request assisted suicide. As discussed in the preceding point, this is a challenging task, requiring considerable effort throughout the healthcare system. Experience in The Netherlands, where there has been relatively little effort to improve pain and symptom treatment, suggests that legalization of physician-assisted suicide might weaken society's resolve to expand services and resources aimed at caring for the dying patient (Foley, 1995; Hendin, 1994). For this reason, the American Pain Society opposes the legalization of

physician-assisted suicide and euthanasia at this time.

5. Laws and regulations must provide protection for health professionals to aggressively treat pain with analgesic drugs, and when needed, with terminal sedation, even if these treatments hasten death. At present, physicians and nurses are often reluctant to give large doses of analgesics to dying patients, fearing that they will be subject to prosecution if the drugs contribute to a respiratory arrest. Regulations must specify that an intent to relieve pain, supported by documentation of the patient's report of pain or behaviors that suggest pain (e.g., grimacing or moaning), can justify the use of high doses of analgesics or sedatives, even if these treatments also depress respiration or hasten death in some other way. Such treatment is based on ethical principles that are widely accepted by health professionals and ethicists (Emanuel, 1998) and should not be considered an act of assisted suicide or euthanasia.

6. We must encourage basic and applied research related to the mechanisms and treatment of symptoms of disease. Medical research has traditionally focused on curing disease, with relatively few resources devoted to improving symptomatic treatment. Over the past 20 years, a small group of basic neuroscientists and clinical researchers have focused on the study of pain. The achievements of this research, including the development of spinal opioid treatment, patient-controlled analgesia, sustained-release opioid compounds, and effective new treatments for pain related to nerve injury and migraine, illustrate the dramatic results that biomedical research can produce when applied to symptom research. Now that treatments exist for many types of pain, a crucial research question is how to ensure their broad application. Many other symptoms of advanced illness have had relatively little basic or clinical research, including poor appetite, fatigue, shortness of breath, constipation, and pain related to the heart, gastrointestinal tract, urinary tract, and female reproductive organs. Governmental and private foundations should encourage the development of research in these areas, with particular attention to training young investigators in specialty areas where there is currently little symptom research.

References

American Pain Society Quality of Care Committee. (1995). "Quality Improvement Guidelines for the Treatment of Acute Pain and Cancer Pain." *Journal of the American Medical Association*, 274, 1874–1880. Cleeland, C.S., Gonin, R., Hatfield, A.K., Edmondson, J.H., Blum, R.H., Stewart, J.A., et al. (1994). "Pain and Its Treatment in Outpatients with Metastatic Cancer." *New England Journal of Medicine*, 330, 592–596. Emanuel, E.J. (1988). "A Review of Ethical and Legal Aspects of Terminating Medical Care." *American Journal of Medicine*, 84, 291–301. Foley, K.M. (1995). "Pain, Physician-Assisted Suicide, and Euthanasia." *Pain Forum*, 4, 163–178. Hendin, H. (1994). "Seduced by Death: Doctors, Patients, and the Dutch Cure." *Issues in Law Medicine*, 10, 123–168. Jacox, A., Carr, D.B., Payne, R., Berde, C.B., Brietbart, W., & Cain, J., et al. (1994). "Management of Cancer Pain." *Clinical Practice Guideline* No. 9. Rockville, MD: U.S. Public Health Service, Agency for Health Care Policy and Research. (AHCPR No. 94-0592.) Max, M.B. (1990). "Improving Outcomes of Analgesic Treatment: Is Education Enough?" *Annals of Internal Medicine*, 113, 885–889.

"Good palliative care [could] be the first choice, with euthanasia as a final option for those whose clinical condition or psychological make-up leads them to decide life is no longer worth living."

Effective Pain Treatment Should Not Rule Out Euthanasia

Bobbie Farsides

In the following viewpoint, Bobbie Farsides argues that effective pain treatment for the terminally ill should not be promoted as the moral alternative to euthanasia. While dying patients should receive the best pain treatments available, euthanasia should be permitted as an option for those whose symptoms do not respond to medical treatments. Those who promote palliative care—compassionate pain relief for the dying—are not necessarily against euthanasia, Farsides points out. Farsides is a lecturer in medical ethics at King's College in London, England.

As you read, consider the following questions:
1. How does the World Health Organization define palliative care?
2. What appears to be the dominant philosophy of palliative care, in Farsides' opinion?
3. Why is it counterproductive to perceive the palliative care movement as anti-euthanasia, in the author's view?

Excerpted from Bobbie Farsides, "Palliative Care—A Euthanasia-Free Zone?" *Journal of Medical Ethics*, June 1998, vol. 24, pp. 149–50. Reprinted with permission from BMJ Publishing Group.

B ritain can be justifiably proud of the part its health care professionals have played in the founding and development of palliative care as a discrete medical and nursing specialty. Individuals and institutions deservedly enjoy worldwide reputations, and practitioners from every continent come here to share in the knowledge-base and expertise that has built up. Slowly the public is becoming more aware of what can be achieved on its behalf by specialist palliative care workers, and this despite the fact that an unacceptably low percentage of the population as yet has access to the full range of services.

What Is Palliative Care?

The World Health Organisation (WHO) defines palliative care as: "the active, total care of patients whose disease is not responsive to curative treatment. Control of pain, other symptoms and psychological, social and spiritual problems is paramount. The goal of palliative care is the achievement of the best quality of life for patients and families."

This definition, combined with the history of the specialty, helps to explain its character. First there is the explicit rejection of the dominant medical model of care, which defines success and failure in relation to cure. Being "other" to this model has allowed practitioners to be responsive to a large range of complementary therapies and to work closely with supporting professions. By including the issue of social and spiritual problems the definition brings to the heart of the agenda concerns which in other areas of medicine are deliberately kept at the periphery. The concept of quality of life is also made central to the idea of appropriate goals of care, and although common to other areas of medicine, for example care of the chronically sick and the disabled, the emphasis is slightly different here, as carers are required to give almost equal consideration to the needs of the patient's family. All these facts contribute to an understanding of palliative care services as inclusive, tolerant, patient/family-centred and forward-looking.

These observations are pretty standard and have been discussed in many different contexts. However, I wish to claim that there is another respect in which palliative care is unusual if not unique, and that is in terms of the moral or ethical views its practitioners propound. When addressing this issue it is interesting to note that this is perhaps the only area of health care that has frequently been characterised as a *movement* (although it has been suggested to me that health promotion has been characterised in a similar way, as have certain strands of psychiatry). Whilst there are certainly movements which have attempted to influence particular areas of medicine, for example the eugenics movement, it is unusual for a medical specialty as a whole to be characterised in terms of a set of non-medical beliefs.

In the case of palliative care reference is often made to "the hospice philosophy" and variants thereof; there is also a perceived link with formal religion uncommon to any other area of medicine. What one seems to encounter in palliative care is a uniformity and explicitness of shared moral beliefs around major ethical issues, which is not reflected in other specialties. Even in specialties such as assisted reproduction and neonatology, which confront profound ethical issues, there is a noticeable difference in terms of the multiplicity of moral views represented, with well-known differences of view around all the major issues such as treatment criteria, commercialisation, abortion etc.

Palliative Care's Dominant Philosophy

In palliative care, despite a very responsible and proactive approach to moral debate there still appears to be a dominant philosophy which some have got close to describing as an ideology. This is not to say that there is total uniformity, there have been very interesting debates recently on matters such as dehydration and rehydration of terminally ill patients, criteria for access to palliative care services, and at a more theoretical level palliative care practitioners have shown willingness to explore their frequent reliance on the doctrine of double effect in the context of pain relief. However, the message on one moral issue, which could arguably be claimed to be *the* moral issue of the moment, always appears to be the same—euthanasia is morally wrong and ought not to be legally acceptable.

This is an interesting observation which invites a number

A False Dichotomy

I applaud the promotion of hospice care in the media. Promoting compassionate palliative care to the general public is essential, especially if one believes that physician-assisted suicide should be made available in the context of offering choices.

But [many do] not promote hospice care as just a choice. [They] promote it as the only moral choice and, in doing so, set up a false dichotomy. . . . One might mistakenly conclude that all proponents of legal reform were either historically naive, ignorant of hospice and palliative care, or both. And while some people may be guilty of this lack of information, many others are not.

Many people who have devoted their lives to the care of the dying are not opposed to physician-assisted suicide. Such people believe it should be available as one of several options, and, therefore, do not believe that promoting hospice, and advocating for the availability of regulated physician-assisted suicide are contradictory goals.

John L. Miller, *American Journal of Hospice and Palliative Care*, May/June 1997.

of possible explanations. First, there is the possibility that the goals and principles of palliative care are logically incompatible with euthanasia. This is certainly how many practitioners feel—being pro-euthanasia is seen as incompatible with being a good palliative care worker. However, when you look at the issue objectively it is difficult to argue this point. The goal of palliative care is to maintain for as long as feasibly possible a *quality* of life. The question then arises as to what is to be done when this can no longer be achieved. Morally and legally there is the option of withdrawal of life-prolonging treatment, which is acceptable to most palliative care practitioners, who would not argue in favour of overenthusiastically prolonging the lives of their patients. This implicitly acknowledges a threshold-type argument relating to quality-of-life considerations, such that below a certain quality a life (rather than the person) loses its value to the extent that it need not be saved, supported or prolonged (assuming that this is the wish of the patient and/or family). But who is to say that this threshold should not be taken to indicate the need for active euthanasia, such that below a certain quality patients should have the right to request that their life be ended?

To deny this possibility one needs to argue independently either that euthanasia is intrinsically morally wrong, most obviously because it is a form of direct killing of the innocent (although here one has the problem that medicine has already accommodated abortion which is even more complex than voluntary euthanasia due to the absence of any known view on the part of the innocent killed), or that the effects of permitting euthanasia are such that it cannot *legally* be permitted whatever its moral status.

An Anti-Euthanasia Lobby?

Members of the palliative care movement have been prominent in offering both types of objections. So prominent in fact that they have increasingly become the media's choice as the obvious anti-euthanasia lobby. Despite the useful and in many cases decisive advice members of the profession have provided to government committees etc, this is not necessarily a desirable position, particularly given the accompanying tendency to present palliative care as *the* alternative to euthanasia thus precluding the need to discuss euthanasia, an extravagant claim which cannot be supported in all cases. Even the existence of a perfect service and complete access to it will not remove the desire on the part of some individuals that their life should end sooner rather than later. At another level, if palliative care is too closely equated with anti-euthanasia views the professions involved could lose some valuable potential entrants, who, for the time being at least would be counting themselves out of a career in this area on the basis of their moral views alone. A third problem might arise in terms of a reluctance on the part of those already in the service to express views counter to those dominant within the group as a whole. However, the most serious problem relates to the most important people in the equation, the patients. One needs to ask to what extent a terminally ill patient (current or potential) who desires euthanasia (irrespective of its legal status) feels marginalised by the philosophy of the palliative care movement.

If euthanasia were to be legalised one would surely want to

avoid presenting patients with an either/or choice between good palliative care and euthanasia. Rather, good palliative care would be the first choice, with euthanasia as a final option for those whose clinical condition or psychological make-up leads them to decide life is no longer worth living. The difficulty is then combining the two in such a way as to allow those who morally object to euthanasia to keep their hands clean. . . .

For as long as the palliative care movement is seen as essentially, definitively anti-euthanasia those patients who desire euthanasia might feel that there is always a choice to be made between effective palliative care and euthanasia, gifted professionals might opt for careers in other specialties, and if it is the case that a broader range of views exists amongst practitioners, we will have lost an opportunity for the type of moral debate from which the truth is most likely to emerge.

> *"The very losses and suffering that seem worst about dying may be the things that allow us to see beyond ourselves to something larger and deeper."*

Suffering Should Not Be Evaded

Kirsten Backstrom

Many people fear the potentially severe pain of terminal illness and assume that such suffering may result in an understandable decision to commit suicide, states Kirsten Backstrom in the following viewpoint. However, Backstrom asserts, deep suffering should not necessarily be avoided. In discussing her painful and life-threatening experience with Hodgkin's lymphoma, Backstrom recalls that physical and emotional suffering did not make her life less rewarding. In fact, she contends, suffering led her to experience rich and profound spiritual insights. Backstrom is a clerk for the Committee for Living with Illness and Loss in Multnomah, Oregon.

As you read, consider the following questions:
1. What physical symptoms did Backstrom experience during her treatments for Hodgkin's lymphoma?
2. What does the author define as her "deeper identity"?
3. In Backstrom's opinion, what is the real danger connected to assisted suicide?

Reprinted from Kirsten Backstrom, "What Quality?" *Friends Journal*, February 1999. Reprinted with permission from the author.

In discussions about death and dying, we often use the phrase "quality of life" as if we all know and agree upon what kinds of qualities are indispensable for our survival and basic happiness. We assume, for instance, that in order to appreciate our lives, we must at least be relatively pain-free, mentally alert, capable of functioning to some extent, and capable of communicating. Based on these assumptions about what a meaningful life must include, it may be dangerously easy to come to the conclusion that life is probably "not worth living" if these essential expectations are not met.

What Is "Quality of Life"?

I want to question some of these most basic ideas about what is necessary for a genuine "quality life." My own experiences with cancer helped me see that many of the preconceptions I had about the value and meaning of my life when I was healthy did not apply at all to my life when I was extremely ill, and probably will not apply when I am dying. While I was undergoing chemotherapy and radiation treatments for Hodgkin's Lymphoma, my "quality of life," by most of the usual standards, would have been considered very low. I was in real pain or extreme discomfort most of the time for many months, suffering from nerve damage, nausea, muscle cramps, mouth sores, headaches, and severe radiation burns on my skin, throat, and esophagus. Eating and sleeping were a struggle rather than a pleasure. My thought processes were slowed and sometimes distorted, my memory weakened, my concentration limited. I was unable to work or to lead any kind of "active life"; in fact, most of my days were spent sitting or lying in my living room, just looking out the window. I communicated less and less, as I focused my energies on inner experiences I could not describe in words. With a life reduced to this extent, it might seem that the only possible comfort would have been found in my positive prognosis: at least I had hopes of an eventual return to health and a "better quality of life."

But, in fact, my experience of this life-threatening illness contradicted all of my assumptions about what was necessary for my "quality of life." Those months of misery, pain, limitation, exhaustion, humiliation, and despair were not empty at all; they were, paradoxically, some of the most meaning-ful, most "high-quality," months of my life. The difficulties were real, the pain was real, the stripping away of identity was very real—yet the opportunity for a new understanding of myself and of God was still more real, pervasive, and pal-pable during this time. When all of the usual standards for a "good life" were gone, other standards emerged. I found that without the things that had superficially defined my life, I still had a life, and one that was filled with richness, won-der, beauty, a kind of grace. It was incredible to discover that my deeper identity—my capacity to feel love and experience joy, my awareness of being part of something larger and more meaningful—did not depend upon physical comfort, the ability to do things in the world, or even the ability to think about things in a particular, familiar way. I was still myself even as my body and my everyday life went to pieces. And I am quite sure that I will still be myself when my body and everyday life ultimately fall away completely as I prepare for death.

Suffering Is Intrinsic to the Human Condition

Perhaps because I have embraced a faith with crucifixion at its heart, I do not consider suffering an aberration or an out-rage to be eliminated at any cost, even the cost of my life. It strikes me as intrinsic to the human condition. I don't like it. I'm not asked to like it. I must simply endure in order to learn from it. Those who leap forward to offer me aid in end-ing it, though they may do so out of the greatest compassion, seek to deny me the fullness of experience I believe I am meant to have.

Nancy Mairs, *Christian Century*, May 6, 1998.

I would never claim that my own experiences should hold true for everyone, but I would encourage myself and others to question our assumptions about what "quality of life" is—for ourselves and for those we love. If we approach the ends of our lives with a terror of losing all of the things we consider essential (our physical control, our faculties, our work and relationships as they are now), then we may prevent ourselves from experiencing what remains, what expands and develops, when we are deprived of these things. If we emphasize that we would like to be "put out of our misery" when we've lost what we now value most, then we deprive ourselves of the possibilities that may lie beyond these values.

While I recognize that persistent pain can make it impossible to appreciate what life still has to offer, I also know from my own experience that it is possible to live fully in the midst of pain, at least for a time. I would like to know that I have the option of dying if pain becomes more than I can bear, but I wouldn't want to decide in advance how much I can bear. This is where, I think, the danger of assisted suicide comes in. We all want to reassure ourselves with the knowledge that we will not be kept alive beyond the point where we can bear to be alive, but from the perspective of relative good health we are not really qualified to judge what we can bear, what is of the deepest value, what comforts and certainties (perhaps spiritual rather than physical) are truly essential to a decent "quality of life."

The Need to Go Beyond Suffering

Often, I believe, when we are extremely ill or dying, we are so frightened by our losses that we do not know how to experience what is actually occurring, what deeper qualities of our lives are emerging. Those who love us, those who are healthy and fear death themselves, see our pain, fear, and distress first and foremost—and because they can only imagine the losses we are going through, they naturally want to do everything in their power to relieve our suffering. But this can have the effect of over-emphasizing the significance of that suffering, making the losses seem too great to tolerate, supporting our fear, and preventing us from going beyond suffering, loss, and fear to whatever else our lives may still hold.

If we have prepared ourselves to believe in the possibility that life is more than the "essential" qualities we've always relied upon, then we might have a very different experience when the time comes to leave those qualities behind. While we are dying there may still be new dimensions of life itself that we have not yet discovered, dimensions that do not depend upon any of the things we think we need, the things we think we are.

It's only reasonable that we should want to know that we will be able to die when we are really ready to die, but it is important that we understand that a person near death may still have "quality of life" even without the capacity to function normally, even in the midst of pain and disorientation, and even, potentially, in a comatose state. We would not want to rush ourselves, or others, through our last, vital experiences simply because we have taught ourselves to assume that life is already over when we have come to this point. The very losses and suffering that seem worst about dying may be the things that allow us to see beyond ourselves to something larger and deeper.

"A federal policy that prohibits physicians from alleviating suffering by prescribing marijuana for seriously ill patients is misguided, heavy-handed, and inhumane."

Marijuana Should Be Legalized for Seriously Ill and Terminally Ill Patients

Jerome P. Kassirer

In the following viewpoint, Jerome P. Kassirer contends that physicians should be allowed to prescribe smokable marijuana for terminally ill patients. Marijuana can inhibit the pain and nausea that sick and dying people often experience, he points out; furthermore, the majority of the public approves of marijuana for such purposes. Kassirer maintains that it is hypocritical and wrong-headed to allow the seriously ill to use pain-killing narcotics such as morphine while simultaneously prohibiting access to therapeutic marijuana. Kassirer is the editor of the *New England Journal of Medicine.*

As you read, consider the following questions:
1. What two states have approved ballot measures legalizing medical marijuana?
2. In Kassirer's opinion, why might smoked marijuana be preferable to dronabinol, the drug that contains marijuana's active ingredient?
3. What is the difference between a Schedule 1 and Schedule 2 drug, according to the author?

The advanced stages of many illnesses and their treatments are often accompanied by intractable nausea, vomiting, or pain. Thousands of patients with cancer, AIDS, and other diseases report they have obtained striking relief from these devastating symptoms by smoking marijuana.[1] The alleviation of distress can be so striking that some patients and their families have been willing to risk a jail term to obtain or grow the marijuana.

Despite the desperation of these patients, within weeks after voters in Arizona and California approved propositions allowing physicians in their states to prescribe marijuana for medical indications, federal officials, including the President, the secretary of Health and Human Services, and the attorney general sprang into action. At a news conference, Secretary Donna E. Shalala gave an organ recital of the parts of the body that she asserted could be harmed by marijuana and warned of the evils of its spreading use. Attorney General Janet Reno announced that physicians in any state who prescribed the drug could lose the privilege of writing prescriptions, be excluded from Medicare and Medicaid reimbursement, and even be prosecuted for a federal crime. General Barry R. McCaffrey, director of the Office of National Drug Control Policy, reiterated his agency's position that marijuana is a dangerous drug and implied that voters in Arizona and California had been duped into voting for these propositions. He indicated that it is always possible to study the effects of any drug, including marijuana, but that the use of marijuana by seriously ill patients would require, at the least, scientifically valid research.

A Misguided Policy

I believe that a federal policy that prohibits physicians from alleviating suffering by prescribing marijuana for seriously ill patients is misguided, heavy-handed, and inhumane. Marijuana may have long-term adverse effects and its use may presage serious addictions, but neither long-term side effects nor addiction is a relevant issue in such patients. It is also hypocritical to forbid physicians to prescribe marijuana while permitting them to use morphine and meperidine to relieve extreme dyspnea and pain. With both these drugs the difference between the dose that relieves symptoms and the dose that hastens death is very narrow; by contrast, there is no risk of death from smoking marijuana. To demand evidence of therapeutic efficacy is equally hypocritical. The noxious sensations that patients experience are extremely difficult to quantify in controlled experiments. What really counts for a therapy with this kind of safety margin is whether a seriously ill patient feels relief as a result of the intervention, not whether a controlled trial "proves" its efficacy.

Sick People Need Relief Now

[Experts have raised] serious questions about the toxicity of marijuana smoke. But many medicines are toxic. The relevant question is, toxic compared to what? The chemicals in chemotherapy are dangerous; so is radiation; so are the drugs in AIDS cocktails. An AIDS patient facing starvation might well be willing to damage his lungs instead. Further work should be done on alternative delivery systems, like inhalers and patches. But in the meantime there are sick people who could use relief now.

Richard Brookhiser, *Marijuana Magazine*, March 22, 1999.

Paradoxically, dronabinol, a drug that contains one of the active ingredients in marijuana (tetrahydrocannabinol), has been available by prescription for more than a decade. But it is difficult to titrate the therapeutic dose of this drug, and it is not widely prescribed. By contrast, smoking marijuana produces a rapid increase in the blood level of the active ingredients and is thus more likely to be therapeutic. Needless to say, new drugs such as those that inhibit the nausea associated with chemotherapy may well be more beneficial than smoking marijuana, but their comparative efficacy has never been studied.

Whatever their reasons, federal officials are out of step with the public. Dozens of states have passed laws that ease restrictions on the prescribing of marijuana by physicians, and polls consistently show that the public favors the use of marijuana for such purposes.[1] Federal authorities should rescind their prohibition of the medicinal use of marijuana for seriously ill patients and allow physicians to decide which patients to treat. The government should change marijuana's status from that of a Schedule 1 drug (considered to be potentially addictive and with no current medical use) to that of a Schedule 2 drug (potentially addictive but with some accepted medical use) and regulate it accordingly. To ensure its proper distribution and use, the government could declare itself the only agency sanctioned to provide the marijuana. I believe that such a change in policy would have no adverse effects. The argument that it would be a signal to the young that "marijuana is OK" is, I believe, specious.

The Rights of Those at Death's Door

This proposal is not new. In 1986, after years of legal wrangling, the Drug Enforcement Administration (DEA) held extensive hearings on the transfer of marijuana to Schedule 2. In 1988, the DEA's own administrative-law judge concluded, "It would be unreasonable, arbitrary, and capricious for DEA to continue to stand between those sufferers and the benefits of this substance in light of the evidence in this record."[1] Nonetheless, the DEA overruled the judge's order to transfer marijuana to Schedule 2, and in 1992 it issued a final rejection of all requests for reclassification.[2]

Some physicians will have the courage to challenge the continued proscription of marijuana for the sick. Eventually, their actions will force the courts to adjudicate between the rights of those at death's door and the absolute power of bureaucrats whose decisions are based more on reflexive ideology and political correctness than on compassion.

References

1. Young FL. Opinion and recommended ruling, marijuana rescheduling petition. Department of Justice, Drug Enforcement Administration. Docket 86-22. Washington, D.C.: Drug Enforcement Administration, September 6, 1988.

2. Department of Justice, Drug Enforcement Administration. Marijuana scheduling petition: denial of petition: remand. (Docket No. 86-22.) Fed Regist 1992; 57(59):10489-508.

"The majority of studies show little or no effectiveness of marijuana when used for medical purposes."

Marijuana Should Not Be Legalized for Seriously Ill and Terminally Ill Patients

Robert L. Maginnis

Medical marijuana should not be legalized, argues Robert L. Maginnis in the following viewpoint. Numerous medical associations and research institutions deny the claim that smoked marijuana provides any benefits for the seriously ill. In fact, Maginnis points out, marijuana smoke is carcinogenic and can damage the immune system. Marinol, an approved drug that contains the synthetic form of marijuana's active ingredient, is a safer and more stable treatment for cancer and AIDS patients, the author concludes. Maginnis is a policy analyst for the Family Research Council, a conservative advocacy organization.

As you read, consider the following questions:
1. According to Maginnis, what four limitations of smoked marijuana make it an ineffective treatment for AIDS wasting syndrome?
2. How does marijuana smoking affect patients with spastic multiple sclerosis, according to the author?
3. Marinol is prescribed to treat what symptoms, according to Maginnis?

Excerpted from Robert L. Maginnis, "Medical Marijuana," *Family Research Council Insight*, 1997. Reprinted with permission from the author.

L egalizing marijuana for medicine deserves a thorough analysis. Advocates say it is a prudent and "compassionate" step for seriously ill patients but the real issue is the legalizing of now-illicit drugs.

On November 5, 1996, the issue of the medical use of marijuana rocketed to national attention via two state propositions. California's "Compassionate Use Act" passed with 56 percent of the vote and permits "seriously ill Californians" to grow, possess and use marijuana legally. The law also permits use for "any other illness for which marijuana provides relief." It protects from prosecution doctors who prescribe marijuana no matter the alleged illness, and the prescription can be either "written or oral." There is no age restriction.

Arizona's "Drug Medicalization, Prevention and Control Act" was packaged as a truth-in-sentencing and drug prevention measure. Buried within the proposition was a provision which allows a physician to prescribe controlled substances like marijuana, heroin, LSD and methamphetamine to "reduce the pain and suffering of the seriously ill and terminally ill."

On December 2, 1996, General Barry McCaffrey, Director, Office of National Drug Control Policy, told the U.S. Senate Judiciary Committee, "The Office of National Drug Control Policy strongly opposes Arizona's Proposition 200 and California's Proposition 215. . . . They both violate the medical-scientific process by which safe and effective medicines are evaluated for use by the medical community. Both measures are actually a quasi-legalization of dangerous drugs. We believe these two measures are unwise and represent a threat to our congressionally approved National Drug Control policy."

Why Oppose Marijuana as Medicine?

Marijuana as medicine is widely rejected despite claims otherwise.

Numerous prestigious medical associations—such as the American Medical Association, the National Multiple Sclerosis Society, the American Glaucoma Society, the American Academy of Ophthalmology and the American Cancer Society—all have rejected the claim that marijuana has any demonstrated medical utility.

A National Institute of Drug Abuse study, entitled "Therapeutic Uses of Cannabis," embodies an exhaustive review of the medical literature. It reveals that the majority of studies show little or no effectiveness of marijuana when used for medical purposes and when its effects are warranted. There are legally approved drugs on the market containing the active ingredient in marijuana.

Their Case: Pro-marijuana forces argue that smoking crude marijuana helps AIDS wasting syndrome patients. The syndrome is characterized by at least a 10 percent weight loss with chronic fever, weakness, or diarrhea in the absence of other related illnesses contributing to the weight loss.

The Facts: Science shows that smoking anything [tobacco or marijuana] doubles the probability of contracting fullblown AIDS for HIV-infected patients and according to the Drug Information Analysis Service, the "efficacy of dronabinol [synthetic THC, marijuana's psychoactive ingredient] in reversing the wasting process in AIDS patients is yet to be determined."

The National Institute on Allergy and Infectious Diseases has identified two commercially available treatments for anorexia/cachexia in patients with AIDS, Megace (magastrol acetate) and Marinol. The Institute dismisses marijuana as an effective AIDS wasting drug by identifying four limitations: drug absorption via smoking may be "impractical or unacceptable;" marijuana includes "a complex mixture of over 400 compounds including polyaeromatic hydrocarbons which are carcinogenic;" marijuana is often contaminated with salmonella and fungal spores which compromise the immune system; and the mind altering effect may distress patients. . . .

Marijuana Is Not an Effective Treatment

Their Case: Marijuana-as-medicine proponents claim that crude pot helps alleviate nausea and vomiting associated with the effects of chemotherapy.

The Facts: In 1996, Harmon J. Eyre, Executive Vice President for Research and Cancer Control for the American Cancer Society stated, there is "no reason to support the legalization of marijuana for medical use."

Joanne Schellenbach, spokeswoman for the American Cancer Society, said her group feels there is "no need to treat the side effects of chemotherapy" with marijuana. There are ample legal pharmaceuticals available to do this which don't present the [medical] problems [caused by] inhaling," she said.

Dr. David S. Ettinger, associate director of the Johns Hopkins Oncology Center, and a nationally respected cancer expert, has written that "There is no indication that marijuana is effective in treating nausea and vomiting resulting from radiation treatment. . . . No legitimate studies have been conducted which make such conclusions."

Anecdotes Should Not Drive Public Health Policy

We must ensure that all patients receive compassionate treatment using medicines proven to be safe and effective. However, the tragic lessons of history serve to remind us that hope and hearsay are not enough. Drug legalization proponents play on the sympathies all Americans share for those suffering from serious illnesses. We must do all that we can to minimize human suffering and to treat these tragic diseases. However, anecdotal claims about the medical benefits of smoked marijuana are insufficient grounds to subvert the protections Americans rely upon and deserve. In short, science provides no reason to exempt smoked marijuana from meeting the same rigorous standards required by all substances purporting to yield medical benefit.

Barry McCaffrey, statement before the House of Representatives, October 1, 1997.

Their Case: Marijuana proponents allege that crude pot can limit the muscle pain and spasticity associated with multiple sclerosis (MS).

The Facts: A 1994 study published in *Clinical Pharmacology & Therapeutics* found that a single marijuana cigarette increased postural tracking error, decreased response speed and further impaired posture and balance. The authors concluded that marijuana smoking impairs coordination and balance in patients with spastic MS.

In 1994, the National Institute of Neurological Disorders and Stroke stated, "There is no evidence that marijuana is effective in modifying the course of MS." The Institute also found that "Marijuana is problematic as a therapy for MS" because "There is no standardized product and method of assuring the bioavailability of its ingredients."

The propositions to legalize marijuana as medicine undermine safe medical procedures.

The Food and Drug Administration (FDA) has a rigorous scientific process for regulating drugs to ensure their safety. Both California and Arizona have bypassed this proven approval process, thereby setting a dangerous precedent.

There is a FDA-approved alternative to marijuana.

A synthetic form of delta-9-tetrahydrocannabinol (THC), the main psychoactive ingredient of marijuana, has been approved by the FDA as an anti-nausea agent for cancer chemotherapy patients and as an appetite stimulant for patients with AIDS Wasting Syndrome. Unlike marijuana, synthetic THC ("Marinol") is a stable, well-defined, pure substance in quantified dosage form.

"[Dying people] need to plan—to think ahead in order to fashion, out of the time remaining, the best of what is possible."

Terminally Ill People Should Plan for the End of Life

Roger C. Bone

Roger C. Bone, a physician who was dying of cancer at the time the following viewpoint was written, offers several suggestions to assist the terminally ill in planning out the rest of their lives. Bone advises dying people to accept help from family and friends and to be assertive in defining wants and needs. He also encourages patients to become informed about their illness and to take advantage of resources and services provided by the health care community.

As you read, consider the following questions:
1. In Bone's opinion, why should terminally ill patients seek a second opinion about their condition?
2. For what reasons are terminally ill patients hospitalized, according to the author?
3. According to Bone, what kinds of nonmedical services do most hospitals provide?

Excerpted from Roger C. Bone, "A Dying Person's Guide to Dying," *Home Care Guide to Advanced Cancer*, 1997. Copyright ©1997 the American College of Physicians. Reprinted with permission.

The central theme of this viewpoint is that planning near the end of life is helpful. By thinking ahead about what could happen—and about how you will deal with problems if they do happen—you can create a better life and a better quality of life for yourself and for the people who love and care about you. What I have to say is for the person who, like myself, is dying. We, too, need to plan—to think ahead in order to fashion, out of the time remaining, the best of what is possible.

As I am dying from cancer, I have learned some things that I think are important for a dying person to know in order to plan. I am a physician, but what I have learned has little to do with my medical training. I have learned this as a person; perhaps my medical experience was helpful because I have paid close attention to the actions and reactions of people around me.

First, it is likely that you will be surrounded by persons who mean well but, in the end, you must die your own death. Dying can be considered a journey one takes alone with a crowd. Family and friends are the first to gather around you, and they offer the most comfort.

After Hearing the Bad News

Here are some pieces of advice to remember in those first few days after you learn the bad news.

1. One or two people—probably family members—will make enormous personal sacrifices to help you. If you are married, your spouse is likely to do this, but don't be surprised if others—a daughter, a brother-in-law, or even a friend, step forward to offer extraordinary help. Be grateful, and accept help, from whatever source, graciously.

2. Some family members, but especially friends, will treat you differently. Even before you show signs of serious illness, people will have a different look in their eyes as they talk with you. You might consider this patronizing or overbearing. It may be difficult, but it is best to ignore their attitudes and treat them as you always have. They will come around to their normal selves when they get over the shock.

3. Happily accept all gifts from family and friends. It makes them feel better and you might receive something

you really like and appreciate.

4. Don't be afraid to ask to be alone. We need time to be by ourselves. Some family and friends may feel driven to fill your every waking moment with activities; perhaps they are trying to "take your mind off" your impending death, but they may also be doing the same thing for themselves.

5. Be your own counsel. No one, including your physician, religious counselor, spouse, or friends can understand 100% what you want and need. It surprised me that some people seemed to "bully" me with advice when they learned that I was terminally ill. We should remember Immanuel Kant's advice to avoid accepting someone else's authority in place of our own powers of reason. We are the ones who should be considering alternatives and making choices. We can, and should, ask for advice. Make telephone calls and read books—but ultimately, we should decide.

6. Slow down and ask your family and friends to slow down. There may not be a lot of time, but there is sufficient time in all but the most extreme cases to think, plan, prepare.

Questions to Ask

There are things you need to know from your doctors and other health care staff. You need not ask all of the following questions or ask them in this order. Still, these questions deal with crucial issues that need to be addressed and, hopefully, resolved.

1. *What is my disease?* You should find out as much as possible about your disease. What is it? How will it affect me? And very importantly, how will it cause my death? First, ask your physician. Additionally, many popular books are available in bookstores and libraries which can give you a basic sense of your disease process and disease terminology. National organizations, such as the American Cancer Society, and often local hospitals can provide brochures, video tapes, or even lay experts to help you and your family understand your particular disease. Ignorance is not bliss; the more you and your family know, the better able everyone will be able to cope with what is happening.

2. *Should I seek a second opinion about my disease and my condition?* Seek a second opinion! A second opinion will relieve

your mind and resolve doubts one way or another that a major mistake has not been made. More importantly, a second opinion will offer a slightly different perspective that may help everyone's understanding. Don't be embarrassed about asking for a second opinion or think that you will make your physician angry. Second opinions are perfectly acceptable, and many physicians are happy when their patients seek second opinions. The original diagnosis is usually confirmed, and you are then more prepared to follow prescribed treatments.

Reprinted by permission of Joel Kauffmann.

3. *What health professional do I especially trust?* Search for and then trust in a single individual. This does not mean you should not listen to all health professionals and follow reasonable directions and advice. But focus on one individual as the final helper. This normally will be the specialist physician in charge of your case.

However, you may know your family doctor better than you know your cancer specialist. If this is the case, your family doctor may be the one to choose. But, if you do, make certain that your family doctor knows that he or she is serving that role.

4. *Why am I going into the hospital?* There are four basic reasons why a terminally ill person would be hospitalized, but not all four necessarily apply to every patient. They are: (a.) to confirm the diagnosis and analyze how far the disease has progressed; (b.) to provide treatment that can only be given in the hospital; (c.) to treat a severe worsening of the disease; and (d.) to treat the final phases of the disease, if this

cannot be done at home or with hospice. You should know which applies to you so that you can understand why things are done to you and what benefits you can expect.

5. *What are the hospital rules about terminally ill patients?* Hospitals and medical centers have written rules and procedures that outline in detail how the hospital will deal with terminally ill patients. These are not "treatment" rules. These protocols or guidelines, as they are called, deal with how to handle end-of-life issues, such as whether the patient (or the patient's family speaking for the patient) wishes extraordinary "heroic" measures to be used to keep the patient alive. Hospitals are obligated, and very willing, to share these protocols or guidelines with patients and families. Consider getting a durable power of attorney in which you name one or two people to make decisions or choices on your behalf if you should be incompetent or incapable of making decisions yourself. Read the "Do Not Resuscitate" policies of the hospital. Death should be peaceful, and you should not ask for anything that gives you prolonged agony.

You should be aware that nurses and other hospital staff may not know that you are terminally ill. This fact may not be written in your chart, which can lead to conflicts between families and hospital staff. The family may assume that everyone in the hospital shares their grief, and will not understand the work-a-day attitude of nurses, dietitians, or others. It is okay for the family to tell the hospital staff that you are dying since they may not know.

Resources for Patients and Families

6. *What resources are available from the health care community?* Most hospitals have many services available to patients and families to help with nonmedical aspects of your care. These include social services and psychological, financial, and religious counseling. For example, a visit, before hospitalization, to the hospital financial counselor by a family member to check on insurance and payment plans is a wise move. In the rush to admit a patient, important information may not get recorded. A 15-minute meeting with counselors can avoid stress and anger over incorrect bills.

Similarly, meeting with the hospital social worker may be

very helpful in arranging home care. Use these services! . . .

7. *What can I do if it seems that nothing is being done or if I don't understand why certain things are done to me?* Hospitals, clinics, and doctors' offices can be confusing places. You can begin to feel you have no control over what is being done to you, and you may wonder if anyone really understands your case. This is the time to call the health professional who is your primary contact—the one you decided you fully trust—your physician specialist or family physician. Ask this person to explain what is going on. Have him or her paged or even called at home if your situation is very upsetting. It is the physician's responsibility to help you, and he or she will not be angry that you called. . . .

8. *How will I and my family pay for my treatment?* Financial professionals employed by hospitals understand billing and what may or may not be covered by Medicare, Medicaid, or private insurance. Consult them and be sure to ask every question to which you and your family need an answer. It is important that you and your family do not panic over billing. Ask for advice and help.

The Hardest Part About Dying

Sometimes the hardest part about dying is the effect it has on your family and friends. Helping them deal with your death helps you find peace and comfort. If you are not at peace with your death, ask the health professional you especially trust to help you find peace. That person will help or will get whatever help is needed. After all, it is the goal of all health professionals, to give you comfort and health during life and peace to you and your family at death.

> *"Much of our society's crisis around death could be said to stem from a lack of awareness of the dying process as a stage of growth."*

Dying Should Be Seen as a Time of Growth

Pythia Peay

The terminally ill would benefit from the recognition that dying can be a time of growth, argues Pythia Peay in the following viewpoint. The end of life offers opportunities for individuals to reconcile with family members and loved ones, discover the meaning of one's life, and develop a deeper spirituality, the author maintains. With guidance from compassionate caregivers, the fatally ill can learn to accept their mortality and die peacefully. Peay is a columnist for Religion News Service and the author of *Putting America on the Couch*.

As you read, consider the following questions:

1. What are the stages of end-of-life growth, according to this viewpoint?
2. According to the author, what is "contemplative caregiving?"
3. In the opinion of Ira Byock, quoted by Peay, what should Americans do to lessen fears about "loss of dignity" among the dying?

Excerpted from Pythia Peay, "A Good Death," *Common Boundary*, September/October 1997. Reprinted with permission from the author.

Like a lightning bolt that sears the sky with illumination, my father's death changed my relationship to life forever. Sitting at his bedside the moment his breathing stopped, I felt I was witnessing a sacred event. As I continued to keep watch, allowing his soul time to depart, I was awed by the transformations in his body: the deep relaxation that smoothed his furrows, the look of pained concentration that slowly changed into wonder, the pearly translucence that softly radiated around him.

However, just as a storm is announced by rumblings of thunder and dark clouds, my father's dying did not happen suddenly. Ten months before he became bedridden, my siblings and I had begun to sense that something in our eccentric and difficult patriarch had changed. Despite his doctor's reassurances that, even with prostate cancer, he had years left, each of us knew instinctively that the end was in sight. We also had a strong hunch that, as in Dylan Thomas's poem, my father would not "go gentle into that good night."

A lifelong drinker and smoker, my father had made it clear that if further treatment became necessary, he would not enter the hospital. If he was going to die, it would happen his way: in bed, with the TV on and a cigarette and a drink nearby. I steeled myself for the worst, imagining that he would die a lonely alcoholic's death or that he would shoot himself if the pain got too severe, as he had often said he might. I relinquished the idea of a funeral because of his hatred of Catholicism, so there would be no end-of-life resolution, I thought sadly—more likely anger, perhaps relief.

But a miracle happened—in fact, a host of them. When my father died, he was at home surrounded by a loving family. He had made his peace with estranged relatives and with God. He had completed his will, reconciled with the Church, and even helped plan a funeral after all. He had spent long hours recalling scenes from his youth, and a steady stream of dreams and hallucinations had opened up for him the possibility of an afterlife. His dying became a kind of party—sending out for his favorite foods, socializing with family, enjoying a few last drinks and cigarettes. And although my father and I did not say all the things to each other I had hoped we might, we walked his very last mile together—and that brought a lasting healing to our relationship.

The miracle of my father's dying occurred not thanks to a divine angel but through the human agency of hospice workers—a chaplain, a social worker, and a nurse—as well as a priest with a soul of gold and a family who maintained a vigil until the end. My father did not die in pain, because he had been treated with morphine; he did not die in fear, because he had confronted his anxieties; and he did not die alone, because, as best he could, he had been helped by counselors to reach closure with those dearest to him.

The American Crisis Around Death

But as the reaction of friends who had also lost parents made clear, my father's dying contrasted dramatically with the cultural norm. The difference, it seemed, stemmed from the hospice support my family had received, so unlike the more clinical treatment in hospital setting. As a result, I began to wonder whether our society's neglect of the metaphysical dimension of death contributes to the suffering that surrounds modern-day dying.

American culture contrasts sharply with that of ancient Egypt, whose enigmatic civilization revolved entirely around the mysteries of death; medieval Europe, with its Christian contemplation of the suffering, crucifixion, and resurrection of Christ; and Tibet, which produced a *Book of the Dead* that mapped out richly detailed landscapes of the afterlife. Aware that death was a central organizing principle of inner and outer life, these cultures did not expect the dying to make the final passage unaided. Instead, priests, priestesses, monks, and nuns provided spiritual and psychological assistance. Such skilled guidance, however, has all but vanished in modern-day America. What was once a royal road traversed by saints and sinners, the powerful and the humble alike, has become a narrowly defined passage involving only the physical dissolution of the body.

Much of our society's crisis around death could be said to stem from a lack of awareness of the dying process as a stage of growth. Just as different steps must be mastered in childhood, adolescence, and adulthood, dying presents its own challenges. Borrowing from the theories of developmental psychologists such as Jean Piaget and Abraham Maslow, Ira Byock, M.D., author of *Dying Well: The Prospect for Growth at the End of Life* and president of the American Academy of Hospice and Palliative Medicine, has conceptualized the landmarks in end-of-life growth: completion of worldly affairs, closure of personal and professional relationships, learning the meaning of one's life, love of oneself and of others, acceptance of the finality of life, sense of a new self beyond personal loss, recognition of a transcendent realm, and surrender to the unknown. When looked at from this perspective, says Christine Longaker, a Buddhist teacher in the Rigpa Fellowship—an international network of centers that follow the teachings of the Buddha—"dying becomes another stage of living, a very vital stage that can allow us to conclude our lives well."

An Art to Be Learned

All of the world's cultures and great religions have considered dying well an art to be learned, an art essential to a good passage into some next life. In fact, nearly every culture before our own secular age has had instructions on the art of dying.

Judaism's mystical teachings on dying and the journey of the soul after death are contained in the esoteric texts of the *Kabbala* and the *Zohar*. The shamanistic rituals of Native American, African, Aborigine, and Latin American cultures are passed down in oral traditions. Asian and Middle Eastern cultures all had sacred rituals and teachings on dying, such as the *Tibetan* and *Egyptian Book of the Dead*.

Marilyn Webb, *The Good Death*, 1997.

Yet the vision of a "good death" in the company of loved ones has been eclipsed by a stormy debate concerning an individual's "right to die" by euthanasia or physician-assisted suicide. The Supreme Court's ruling that physician-assisted suicide is not a constitutional right but should be decided by state governments means that the issue is unlikely to vanish. Some call it the abortion debate of the twenty-first century.

In part because of this controversy, there is a renewed commitment among many to encourage hospice and other forms of "contemplative caregiving"—those that attend to not only the physical but also the emotional and spiritual needs of the dying. Much as Baby Boomers transformed the way America receives obstetrical care, Byock hopes that, as they care for dying parents, friends, and even children, they will transform how Americans die as well. "We depathologized the concept of pregnancy and birth, saying that it was not a disease but a part of healthy living," he explains. "Similar things can be said about the end of life: that we need not pathologize people in order to acknowledge their mortality. In fact, people can become healthy in their dying.". . .

Physical and Emotional Suffering

When asked what he does as a hospice physician to help people work on the spiritual aspects of their lives, Byock says that he first treats their physical pain. "I help them deal with their bowels," he says. "If they don't do it, trust me, they won't be thinking about what meaning their life had; they'll be worried about their bowels. Only when he or she is comfortable enough can a dying person's attention be drawn to end-of-life issues.". . .

As difficult as it can be to ease the physical pain of the dying, most caregivers agree that psychological anguish is far more challenging to treat. . . .

Dale Borglum, director of the Living/Dying Project in Fairfax, California, tells the story of a woman dying of a brain tumor who had made an agreement with her husband that if she got sick enough and wanted to die, he would help her. But when she decided it was time, her husband had changed his mind. Borglum was called in to mediate.

"When I asked her why she wanted to end her life," Borglum recalls, "she said it was because she was burdening those she loved. When I asked her husband and her other caregiver if she was a burden to them, they both said it was a privilege and an honor to care for her and that they hoped she would live as long as possible. Then she started crying, realizing that it wasn't that she wanted to die but that she had felt like a burden. She died just two days later, but if her husband had given her the drugs he would have felt bad. This way there was a great deal of closure."

Loss of dignity is another cause of suffering for the dying.

Such a fear, notes Byock, is a cultural problem. "As a national community," he says, "all of us need to say loudly that we do not consider people to be undignified or abhorrent because of their physical frailty or dependence." Byock compares caring for dying people to caring for infants. "We would not consider an infant to be in any way undignified by his or her complete physical dependence and incontinence. Even a colicky baby, who cries continuously, is not left in isolation. What do we do with that child? We respond with unconditional loving and care, not just as a family but as a community."

Compounding feelings of depression and loss of dignity is the anguish that occurs when the dying look back on the negative aspects of their lives: the failure of relationships, the hurt inflicted upon others, the missed opportunities, the questions of identity and meaninglessness. Yet, say contemplative caregivers, dying consciously can bring insight into the true nature of personal suffering. For while too much physical suffering can halt soul development, bearing emotional pain can yield enormous spiritual growth. To help extract the gold from the dark of suffering, most religions have cultivated a body of wisdom that can be used to illuminate the soul work of the dying. Joan Halifax, who has studied several forms of Buddhism since the mid-'60s and is an ordained lay priest in Vietnamese monk Thich Nhat Hanh's Tiep Hien Order, draws a distinction between pain and suffering: "Pain is the sensation of extreme discomfort, and suffering is the 'story,' or our feelings toward it."

Forgiveness

As the emotional scars pitting every human heart attest, suffering is in great part related to the pain caused by interpersonal relationships. And the people who have hurt us the most, says Halifax, are usually those we love. But, she says, "meditation teaches us that we are in an ever-changing river of feelings, thoughts, and sensations. Relationships reflect this transient nature of reality: One day you love someone, the next day you're angry with them, and the next moment you're good friends. So to die feeling as though the condition of hurt or betrayal is permanent is tragic."

According to contemplative caregivers, meditations on forgiveness help prevent this kind of tragedy. In fact, forgiveness is considered one of the essential tasks in the "life review"—the reflection on the events and relationships of a lifetime—that is part of conscious dying. Often, forgiveness occurs naturally on the deathbed as what once caused anger dissolves in light of the bigger picture of death. Sister Sharon Burns, for instance, says that she has seen hospice patients reconcile at the last moment over the phone with estranged children or siblings.

Of course, often people cannot forgive others because to do so would be to condone unforgivable transgressions. But one needs to distinguish between an act and the person who committed it, says Levine: "The quality of forgiveness is never a quality of condoning. You never forgive an act such as abuse, theft, or mistreatment. But you can forgive someone whose heart, for that moment, could not see."

The Question of Meaning

Perhaps one of the most tragic kinds of suffering the dying must grapple with is the feeling that their lives lacked meaning. In these instances, it is up to hospice caregivers not to provide pat spiritual answers but rather to listen unconditionally to the dying's life reviews. By asking questions, or simply reflecting back to the dying their own words, the caregivers may allow a pattern of meaning to emerge.

Burns tells the story of a 61-year-old dying woman who, although comfortable with her atheism, was deeply troubled by the question of whether her life had meant anything. "Could you say that the world has been left a little better because you've been here?" Burns recalls asking her patient. "Or that you've made a difference?" Immediately, the woman's husband chimed in about the many political, social, and community organizations she had belonged to, prompting his wife to reminisce about her marriage and children. Eventually, Burns says, the woman came to see that her life had indeed been worthwhile; having let go of her anxieties, she died at peace.

Many of the dying, however, are unable to find anything of value in their life. Drawing on workshops he gave in Los

Angeles, Levine describes in his book the poignancy of some participants with life-threatening illnesses who, as "out-of-work actors lost in the miasma of Hollywood hell," realized that they would never achieve their life's ambition. But caregivers stress that it is never too late to find meaning in life. All of us, Longaker writes, "yearn to do one noble act" before we die. She lists certain final acts that the dying person might consider, such as donating an organ, changing one negative pattern, asking forgiveness for past harm, or making offerings to religious or charitable organizations. . . .

What Comes After?

While there are many techniques and practices to help both the dying and their loved ones achieve acceptance and completion with regard to the conclusion of their life, what of the unknown future that the dying are about to move into? What, if anything, of themselves will remain? Not knowing the answers to these questions can be a major source of anxiety and distress. Despite his belief in the afterlife, even author M. Scott Peck admits that "it's scary to go on an adventure where you don't know where you may be going." Peck says his outspokenness comes as a relief to many Christians who believe they should have no fear of death. "It's normal and healthy to be afraid," he says. "I would worry about someone who had no fear of dying."

While a fear of death should be respected, such fears should not prevent people from exploring their beliefs about the afterlife. Indeed, confronting what some call the "psychospiritual" distress around dying forms the last two of the developmental tasks formulated by Byock: recognition of a transcendent realm and surrender to the unknown. To help caregivers assist the dying in this process, psychotherapist Elizabeth Smith, an associate professor of social work at the Catholic University of America in Washington, D.C., has developed a "transegoic" model of intervention based on the work of transpersonal psychologists like Roger Walsh, M.D., and Frances Vaughan, as well as the late Swiss psychiatrist Carl Jung.

The psychological tasks involved in dying, explains Smith, are counter to the direction individuals have moved in all their lives—the construction of an individual ego identity that psychologists say is the definition of good mental health. But while strong attachment and identity formation may be the norm for healthy psychological development of the living, "ego disattachment" and the development of a "personal death perspective," she says, are the work of the dying.

In an article in the journal the *National Association of Social Workers*, Williams describes how clinicians can help patients move through the process of disidentification with the ego and reidentification with a transpersonal, or higher, self. Among other exercises, patients practice letting go of the roles that once defined them and that are naturally falling away in death—lawyer, bachelor, mother, musician—then identifying with the "I" that remains and "just is." Or those who have trouble leaving behind an earthly talent, such as playing the piano, might conceive of carrying the essence of music onward within their spirit. Similarly, as the body disintegrates from the effects of illness, caregivers might ask their clients, "Are you your hair?" or "Are you your breast?" Cultivating consciousness for what remains, they might then ask the client if she ever had a mystical experience of union with the universe or a sense of what her future might be after death.

Other caregivers, however, say they rarely bring up questions of the afterlife unless specifically asked. As a kind of religious protocol, they are respectful of not proselytizing or imposing upon the dying person their own beliefs. If they are asked, these caregivers are careful to inquire about the person's religious beliefs and to respond in ways that respect such beliefs: A Christian caregiver, for instance, would not talk about Jesus and the resurrection to a Jew but would encourage exploring the religious images of the person's own tradition—such as the Tree of Life in the kabbalah.

Mostly, however, contemplative caregivers say they assist the dying spiritually by centering their work within the practices of their own tradition in order to create a sacred atmosphere. "There's not much you can explain," says Halifax, "but there's a lot you can *be*." When visiting a dying person, she says she leaves all her manuals, books, training, and ideas at the door and listens to "what their hearts know."

Periodical Bibliography

The following articles have been selected to supplement the diverse views presented in this chapter. Addresses are provided for periodicals not indexed in the *Readers' Guide to Periodical Literature*, the *Alternative Press Index*, the *Social Sciences Index*, or the *Index to Legal Periodicals and Books*.

James F. Bresnahan   "Palliative Care or Assisted Suicide?" *America*, March 14, 1998.

Ira Byock   "Suicide Debate Is Still off Course," *Truth Seeker*, vol. 126, no. 1, 1999. Available from 16935 W. Bernardo Dr., Suite 103, San Diego, CA 92127.

R. Henry Capps Jr.   "Physician-Assisted Suicide or Palliative Care?" *Phi Kappa Phi Journal*, Spring 1998.

Consumer Reports   "Marijuana as Medicine: How Strong Is the Science?" May 1997.

Dan Dugan   "When Suffering Is More than Physical Pain," *Park Ridge Center Bulletin*, September/October 1997. Available from 211 E. Ontario, Suite 800, Chicago, IL 60611.

Nancy Mairs   "Learning from Suffering," *Christian Century*, May 6, 1998.

Richard John Neuhaus   "Born Toward Dying," *First Things*, February 2000. Available from 156 Fifth Ave., Suite 400, New York, NY 10010.

Christina M. Puchalski   "Spirituality and Medicine," *World & I*, June 1998. Available from 3600 New York Ave. NE, Washington, DC 20002.

Jonathan Rosen   "Rewriting the End: Elisabeth Kübler-Ross," *New York Times Magazine*, January 22, 1995.

George P. Smith II   "Terminal Sedation as Palliative Care: Revalidating a Right to a Good Death," *Cambridge Quarterly of Healthcare Ethics*, Fall 1998. Available from Cambridge University Press, 40 West 20th St., New York, NY 10011-4211.

Arnold Trebach and Joseph A. Califano Jr.   "Medical Marijuana," *World & I*, March 1997. Available from 3600 New York Ave. NE, Washington, DC 20002.

CHAPTER 3

Should Physicians Be Permitted to Hasten the Deaths of Terminally Ill Patients?

Chapter Preface

Many of the medical and technological tools that can prolong the life or ease the pain of the terminally ill provoke controversy, because certain medical choices may also shorten the lives of patients. The question of retaining or withdrawing nutritional life support for dying patients, for example, reveals sharp differences of opinion within the medical community and among the general public.

The provision of food and fluids by tube is a common form of life support for weak, injured, or unconscious patients. Tube feeding is of great benefit to burn victims and to people recovering from surgery and serious intestinal disorders. However, some experts do not believe that nutritional life support is appropriate for patients in the last stages of terminal illness. In fact, they argue, tube feeding often prolongs the dying process and increases the agony during the last days of a patient's life. Since a dying person eventually loses the desire for food, some medical personnel contend that the withdrawal of feeding tubes allows the dying process to progress naturally and painlessly.

Others, however, disagree that the removal of nutritional life support always alleviates suffering for the dying. One woman who saw her cancer-stricken brother die after his feeding tubes were removed states that "while he was still able to feel pain, he was racked by agonizing muscle spasms. When he was finally dead, he was so contorted that the undertaker was unable to make him presentable." It is impossible for healthy people to really know how it feels to starve to death, some argue, so physicians and caregivers should not invite the increased suffering or premature death that could result from the withdrawal of feeding tubes.

Whether physicians should prolong terminally ill patients' lives or hasten their deaths continues to be one of the most challenging questions in medical ethics today. The authors of the following chapter debate issues regarding life support, narcotic prescriptions, and euthanasia.

*"Legally, artificial nutrition and hydration
is considered a medical treatment that may
be refused at the end of life."*

Withdrawing Life Support Is Acceptable

Choice in Dying

Tube feeding is a common form of life-sustaining treatment
for patients who are unable to eat or drink on their own. In
the following viewpoint, Choice in Dying, a national organization dedicated to serving the needs of the dying, maintains that it is acceptable to withdraw nutritional life support from the terminally ill. In fact, avoiding tube feeding
often allows for a less painful and more comfortable death,
the organization points out. Those who want to refuse nutritional life support when they are close to death should
make their wishes known in advance to ensure that caregivers will honor them.

As you read, consider the following questions:

1. What are the side effects of artificial nutrition and
   hydration, according to Choice in Dying?
2. How long does it take for terminally ill people to die
   after nutritional life support is withdrawn, according to
   the authors?
3. In the authors' opinion, what has been nature's way of
   relieving suffering for the dying?

Excerpted from Choice in Dying, "Artificial Nutrition and Hydration and End-
of-Life Decision-Making," pamphlet, 1994. Reprinted with permission from
Partnership for Caring, 1035 30th St., NW, Washington, DC 20007, 1-800-989-
9455.

What is artificial nutrition and hydration? Artificial nutrition and hydration is a form of life-sustaining treatment. It is a chemically balanced mix of nutrients and fluids, provided by placing a tube directly into the stomach, the intestine or a vein.

When is it used? Artificial nutrition and hydration is given to a person who for some reason cannot eat or drink enough to sustain life or health. Without nutrition and fluids a person will eventually die. Artificial nutrition and hydration is a medical treatment that allows health care providers to bypass whatever may be preventing a person from eating or drinking. It may be used for a variety of conditions. Short-term artificial nutrition and hydration often is given to patients recovering from surgery, greatly improving the healing process. It may also be given to people with increased nutritional requirements, such as burn victims, or to someone who cannot swallow because of an obstructing tumor. A highly sophisticated form of artificial nutrition and hydration (total parenteral nutrition or TPN) can be given indefinitely. For example, TPN can be given to patients with serious intestinal disorders that impair their ability to digest food, enabling them to live fairly normal lives. However, long-term artificial nutrition and hydration also is commonly given to people with irreversible neurological disorders, such as advanced Alzheimer's Disease or severe stroke, although it cannot reverse the condition or change the course of the disease itself.

How is it given? Artificial nutrition and hydration may be given in several ways. Usually it is provided through a flexible tube inserted through the nasal passage into the stomach (nasogastric or NG tube), through the wall of the abdomen into the stomach (gastrostomy, G tube or PEG) or into the intestine (jejunostomy). Insertion through the wall of the abdomen requires a minor surgical procedure. TPN requires the surgical insertion of a special catheter or port, usually into a vein below the collar bone. Fluid with limited amounts of nutrients (or fluids alone) can be supplied directly into a vein in the arm through an intravenous (IV) line. Nutrition and hydration may be supplied temporarily, until the person recovers the ability to eat and drink, or indefinitely. If artificial nutrition is likely to be given for a long time or permanently, a surgically implanted tube is generally more comfortable for the patient and has fewer side effects.

Side Effects of Tube Feeding

Are there side effects from artificial nutrition and hydration? Yes. A number of side effects may occur, especially with the long-term use of artificial nutrition and hydration. Tubes can damage and erode the lining of the nasal passage, esophagus, stomach or intestine. If tube placement requires surgery, complications such as infection or bleeding may arise. Intravenous lines can become uncomfortable if the insertion site becomes infected or if fluid leaks into the skin causing inflammation or infection. Intravenous fluids must be given with extra care to frail patients in order to avoid fluid overload and serious breathing difficulties. TPN requires particular skill and care to ensure that dangerous infections do not enter the blood stream.

Many patients receiving artificial nutrition and hydration by NG or G-tube have brain disease and are unable to report that they feel full or unwell, so abdominal bloating, cramps or diarrhea may occur. Regurgitation is common, and the feed (the nutritional substance inserted through the tube) may be inhaled into the lungs causing pneumonia.

With careful attention by health care providers, many side effects can be avoided or managed fairly well. However, confused patients also can become anxious over a tube's presence and try to pull it out. This often leads to the use of restraints—tying the patient's arms down—or to sedation, which can have a serious effect on patients' mental state and their ability to interact or to perform any small activities they might be capable of, such as changing position in bed.

Is artificial nutrition and hydration different from ordinary eating and drinking? Yes. An obvious difference is that providing artificial nutrition and hydration requires technical skill. Professional skill and training is necessary to insert the tube and to make decisions about how much and what type of feed to give. Skilled management is also required to limit bad side effects.

Other important differences exist. Artificial nutrition and

hydration does not offer the sensory rewards and comforts that come from the taste and texture of food and liquids. Doctors and nurses, rather than patients themselves, control when and how much will be "eaten." Finally, the social interaction that often accompanies eating and drinking is not present.

For patients at the end of life, providing artificial nutrition and hydration may prolong the dying process, without contributing to the patient's comfort. In fact, because of side effects, artificial nutrition and hydration may actually contribute to the dying patient's discomfort.

To some, these differences do not matter because the provision of any type of nourishment and fluids to a sick person is considered an important act of caring that overrides any differences between artificially supplied nutrition and hydration and the provision of ordinary food and water. To others, however, artificial nutrition and hydration is a medical treatment that is vastly different from ordinary eating and drinking. Because people can have such different views about artificial nutrition and hydration, it is important that individuals let others know their views.

A More Comfortable Death

Will the withdrawal of artificial nutrition and hydration lead to a long and painful death? No. For patients who are at the end of life, death normally occurs within three to fourteen days after artificial nutrition and hydration is stopped (the time varies depending on how debilitated the patient was when treatment was discontinued). Reports based on the observation of unconscious patients indicate that the process is quite peaceful, and no evidence exists that they are aware of the process. Conscious patients who are elderly or neurologically impaired usually will slip quickly into a coma (a sleeplike state that is inherently free of pain) and become similarly unaware.

Caregivers of the dying and patients themselves have reported that those who are near death are seldom hungry, and if feelings of hunger occur, small amounts of food by mouth are usually all the patient wants. The most common complaint is dry month, a condition that can be alleviated by sips of water, ice chips, lubricants for the lips or other appropriate oral care. On rare occasions, patients may experience twitching or muscle spasms when hydration is withdrawn, but these symptoms can be managed easily with sedatives. Symptoms that sometimes occur, such as severe pain or nausea, are due to the disease itself. Supplying artificial nutrition and hydration will not alleviate these symptoms and may even make them worse.

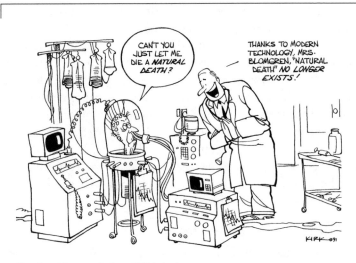

Reprinted by permission of Kirk Anderson.

Is there evidence that avoiding artificial nutrition and hydration contributes to a more comfortable death? Yes. Much of this evidence is based on observations by those who have had a great deal of experience caring for the dying, such as hospice workers. They have noticed that patients who are not tube fed seem more comfortable than those who are. Caregivers also have observed that symptoms such as nausea, vomiting, abdominal pain, incontinence, congestion, shortness of breath, among others, decreased when artificial nutrition and hydration were discontinued making the patient more comfortable. For example, patients with pneumonia, one of the most common terminal events among the elderly or people with terminal illness, will not suffer as much from coughing or shortness of breath due to excess mucous production if they are not receiving fluids. Medical observation has found no indications that patients who have suffered massive brain damage causing permanent unconsciousness experience any pain when artificial nutrition and hydration is stopped.

Reports from conscious dying patients indicate that they increasingly experience a lack of appetite and thirst. In fact, it is common for competent hospice patients and those suffering acute illness to refuse food and water. Dry mouth is the only commonly reported symptom, and this can be managed without resorting to tubes.

Animal studies indicate that the body responds to a lack of food by increasing the production of natural pain relievers (endorphins). However, if food is supplied, the body stops producing endorphins and the benefit of this natural pain relief is lost.

Artificial nutrition and hydration is largely a 20th century technology. Historically, coma was nature's way of relieving the suffering of the dying. However, the provision of artificial nutrition and hydration may prevent the development of this natural anesthesia in some cases.

Is it ever appropriate to give artificial nutrition and hydration to patients who are at the end of life? Yes. As with any medical treatment, tube feeding and hydration should be given if they contribute to overall treatment goals for the patient. These treatment goals should always focus on the patient's wishes and interests. If the goal is to keep the patient alive, then artificial nutrition and hydration may be essential treatment. But if the goal is to provide comfort care *only*, artificial nutrition and hydration usually is not appropriate and may actually add to the person's discomfort.

Some individuals from personal or religious conviction may believe that nutrition and fluids always must be given no matter what the condition or prognosis, or how much the patient may be suffering. Because the provision of food and water can have enormous symbolic significance for some, it can have a powerful effect on decisions about the provision of artificial nutrition and hydration. If the symbolic importance exists for the patient, caregivers should respect the patient's wishes to continue treatment. However, if the symbolic importance exists for the family and caregivers, but not necessarily for the patient, the decision to continue artificial nutrition and hydration may need closer examination. . . .

Legal Questions

What does the law say about artificial nutrition and hydration? Legally, artificial nutrition and hydration is considered a medical treatment that may be refused at the end of life. If the patient still has the capacity to make decisions, the patient can tell the physician what he or she wants. However, for patients who are too sick to communicate, certain states demand strong evidence that a patient would choose to refuse treatment before the state will permit treatment to be stopped.

Every state law allows individuals to refuse artificial nutrition and hydration through the use of an advance directive such as a living will or durable power of attorney for health care, which is used to appoint an agent or surrogate to speak for the patient. However, state laws vary as to what must be done to make wishes known. In many states nutrition and hydration is simply considered a medical treatment that may be refused in an advance directive. But in some states individuals are required to state specifically whether or not they would want artificial nutrition and hydration at the end of life. When uncertainty or conflict exists about whether or not a person would want the treatment, treatment usually will be continued.

Because caregivers' own views may be very different from the patient's views, even if state law does not require it, it is wise for people to make their wishes about the use of artificial nutrition and hydration known in advance and to be sure that caregivers will honor them. Some states prohibit caregivers or agents from making decisions to stop the use of artificial nutrition and hydration unless they specifically know the patient's own wishes. Carefully read the instructions that come with the advance directives or contact Choice in Dying for information about the state's law. . . .

Is it considered a suicide to refuse artificial nutrition and hydration? No. When a person is refusing life-sustaining treatment at the end of life, including artificial nutrition and hydration, it is not considered an act of suicide. A person at the end of life is dying, not by choice, but because of a particular condition or disease. Continuing treatment may delay the moment of death but cannot alter the underlying condition.

Are life insurance policies affected if life-sustaining treatments are refused? No. Because death is not the result of a suicide, life insurance policies are not affected when medical treatments are stopped and the patient is permitted to die.

Does the medical community agree that it is ethically permissible to stop artificial nutrition and hydration? Professional organizations such as the American Academy of Neurology, American Medical Association, American Nurses Association, American Thoracic Society and Society of Critical Care Medicine have affirmed through policy statements that artificial nutrition and hydration are medical treatments and their use should be evaluated in the same way that any other treatment would be. Other major organizations that have issued similar policy statements or treatment guidelines include The American Dietetic Association and the Alzheimer's Association. However, some doctors and nurses personally believe that it is never appropriate to withhold or stop artificial nutrition and hydration. It is therefore important that individuals discuss their wishes with their physician and confirm that their wishes will be honored. . . .

Watching someone we love die makes us feel powerless. But even when "nothing can be done" to cure the disease, there is a great deal that can be done to make the person's last days comfortable and even productive and meaningful. As we broaden our understanding of providing care to the dying, we are improving the management of pain and other symptoms. Through the exceptional work of the hospice movement, we have come to recognize that care of the dying requires medical expertise and a collaborative approach among all of a patient's caregivers. This collaboration allows caregivers to consider the total needs of the patient. Because of the powerful symbolism that associates the provision of food and water with caring, we as caregivers (family and professional), may be uncomfortable about withholding artificial nutrition and hydration. It is important to remember that when we are entrusted with decisions about the care of the dying, the patient's comfort and wishes must guide our decisionmaking, not our own.

*"That [the withdrawal of food and water]
will be replaced by a painless injection or
death pill is a foregone conclusion."*

Acceptance of the Withdrawal of Life Support Could Lead to the Acceptance of Euthanasia

Charles E. Rice

The decision to withdraw feeding tubes and hydration from vegetative patients is often questionable, maintains Charles E. Rice in the following viewpoint. Although the fatally ill should be allowed to die, some comatose or severely disabled patients have had life support withdrawn even though they still had many years to live. Moreover, Rice contends, death by starvation and dehydration is a gruesome process that is difficult to watch. Because of this, many are willing to endorse euthanasia for the terminally ill, believing that such intentional killing is more humane than withdrawal of nutritional life support. However, the law should forbid any purposeful killing of the innocent, Rice concludes. Rice is a professor at Notre Dame Law School.

As you read, consider the following questions:
1. Why should Nancy Cruzan not have had her feeding tube removed, in Rice's opinion?
2. According to Justice Lynch, quoted by the author, what are the specific physical effects of starvation and dehydration?
3. According to the Harris poll cited in this viewpoint, what percent of the population believes that the terminally ill should have access to lethal prescriptions?

Reprinted from Charles E. Rice, "America's Death Wish," *The New American*, January 5, 1998. Reprinted with permission from *The New American*.

In 1994, 51 percent of Oregon voters approved the Death With Dignity Act. In 1997, they rejected, by a 60-40 margin, a proposal to repeal the Act. Court challenges are expected, but the latest result has prompted efforts to enact similar laws in other states.

The Oregon Act provides that a "capable" adult, "determined by [two physicians] to be suffering" from an "incurable and irreversible" terminal disease that will "produce death within 6 months," "may make a written request for medication [to end] his or her life in a humane and dignified manner." The patient must also make "an oral request . . . and reiterate [it] to [the] attending physician no less than 15 days after making the initial oral request." The Act does not authorize any person "to end a patient's life by lethal injection, mercy killing or active euthanasia."

In assisted suicide, the physician, by prescribing or administering a lethal drug or treatment, intentionally and actively helps the patient kill himself. The Supreme Court in 1998, in *Washington v. Glucksberg* and *Vacco v. Quill*, upheld laws forbidding assisted suicide and left open the constitutionality of laws, like the Oregon Act, which allow it.

"Letting" or "Making"

In *Vacco v. Quill*, the lower court had held unconstitutional New York's prohibition against assisted suicide because terminal patients "on life-support systems are allowed to hasten their deaths by directing the removal of such systems; but those [not on] life-sustaining equipment, are not allowed to hasten death by self-administering prescribed drugs." But the Supreme Court upheld the prohibition on the ground that making such a "distinction between assisting suicide and withdrawing life-sustaining treatment . . . is certainly rational."

The Court in *Vacco* relied on its 1990 *Missouri v. Cruzan* decision to support its "distinction between letting a patient die and making that patient die." In *Cruzan* the Court held that Missouri could require "clear and convincing" evidence of Nancy Cruzan's intent not to be sustained on a feeding tube before it would permit removal of that tube. On rehearing, such evidence was found and the tube was withdrawn.

There comes a time when nature should take its course,

the proper judgments of physicians and family should be respected, and the patient should be allowed to die a natural and dignified death. But Nancy Cruzan had a life expectancy of 30 years. Her feeding tube sustained her life, even though it would not correct her underlying condition. Twelve days after removal of the food and water, she died. The official cause of death was "shock due to dehydration due to traumatic brain injury." But the "dehydration" was caused, not by the earlier brain injury Nancy had suffered in an accident, but by the lack of water due to the removal of the tube. The Missouri Supreme Court had it right when it said that "this is not a case in which we are asked to let someone die. . . . This is a case in which we are asked to allow the medical profession to make Nancy die by starvation and dehydration."

The state is morally obliged to forbid the intentional killing of the innocent. That protection should include the terminally ill and those who have asked to be killed.

Terminal Sedation?

In *Vacco*, the Court said that a state "may prohibit assisting suicide while permitting patients to refuse . . . lifesaving treatment [and] it may permit palliative care . . . which may have the . . . unintended 'double effect' of hastening the patient's death. . . . [W]hen a doctor provides . . . palliative care . . . the physician's purpose and intent is, or may be, only to ease his patient's pain." "Palliative care" includes what the Supreme Court referred to as "terminal sedation."

Dr. Timothy Quill, the physician who brought the *Vacco* case, stated in April 1997, "Physician-assisted suicide is a bad option. . . . [T]he practice of sedating a dying patient to the point they either stop breathing or die of dehydration . . . is a better option." While the physician's intent in such cases may be to relieve pain, it could instead be to kill. It is very difficult for the law to distinguish cases in which pain-relieving palliatives and sedation are used for proper medical reasons from cases in which they are used with intent to kill.

We can expect officials and courts to defer to medical judgment in such cases, barring exceptional circumstances. This will enable physicians to sedate their willing patients to death as long as the physicians are circumspect about it. The experience in Holland, where active assisted suicide is tolerated, indicates that such practices will not be limited to willing patients, but will be extended to others who, in the physician's judgment, would be better off dead, including incompetents who will have the desire to die attributed to them. "The 1990 Remmelink Report by Dutch researcher P.J. van der Maas found involuntary euthanasia in 30.76 percent of the cases studied," the November 4, 1997 *Washington Times* reported. "The *New England Journal of Medicine* published a 1995 study by him in which 22.5 percent of euthanized patients had not given doctors their consent."

It is also difficult for the law to determine whether the intent is to kill when the technique is not sedation but the withdrawal of nutrition and hydration. Competent patients are allowed by the law to starve and dehydrate themselves to death. As to incompetents, *Cruzan* allowed withdrawal of food and water from a "vegetative" patient who was not dying, was not in significant discomfort, and had a life expectancy of 30 years.

Withdrawal of Feeding Tubes Will Not Endure

Withdrawal of food and water, however, will not endure as a usual technique for intentional killing of patients. In the 1986 Massachusetts *Brophy* case, Justice Lynch, dissenting from the withdrawal of food and water from an incompetent vegetative patient, said that this would cause a "difficult, painful and gruesome death," and "the cause of death would not be some underlying physical disability." "Why not use more humane methods of euthanasia if that is what we endorse?" he asked.

Justice Lynch recounted the evidence in the case as to the usual effects of starvation and dehydration: "Brophy's mouth would dry out and become caked or coated with thick material. . . . His tongue would swell, and might crack. His eyes would recede back into their orbits and his cheeks would become hollow. The lining of his nose might crack and cause his nose to bleed. His skin would hang loose on his body and become dry and scaly. His urine would become highly concentrated, leading to burning of the bladder. The lining of his stomach would dry out and he would experience dry heaves and vomiting. His body temperature would become very high. His brain cells would dry out, causing convulsions. His respiratory tract would dry out, and the thick secretions . . . could plug his lungs and cause death. . . . [H]is major organs, including his lungs, heart, and brain, would give out and he would die." Paul Brophy died eight days after his feeding was terminated; the stated cause of death was "pneumonia."

The Removal of Feeding Tubes Causes Suffering

Starvation and dehydration do cause suffering. They add to the cruelty and ugliness of death and reinforce the idea that the helpless person is no longer a member of the human family. I am sure that some will say that the sufferings of thirst and starvation can be alleviated, but it is asking a great deal of nurses and doctors to expect them to take away food and water and then treat the problems caused by taking away food and water. And if some compassionate doctors or nurses make an effort to discover effective sedation to remove the torments of thirst, if they try to keep the patient's electrolytes balanced and carefully adjust the amount of food and fluid (still using the feeding tube) in order to lessen the suffering as much as possible, then nature is no longer allowed to take its course.

Nancy Harvey, *First Things*, April 1995.

Obviously, this is a difficult way to die, and a difficult death to witness. That such means of demise will be replaced by a painless injection or death pill is a foregone conclusion. In a Harris poll in 1997, 68 percent of those queried answered "yes" when asked if terminally ill people should be allowed to obtain a lethal prescription.

The Future Is Now

The Supreme Court has already invited the states to turn a blind eye to euthanasia committed under the guise of legitimate palliative care, sedation, or withdrawal of treatment. Active euthanasia will predictably follow. Nor will euthanasia be limited to consenting patients. Rising costs will induce families and physicians to opt for termination of life of the incompetent, the aged, and the disabled. This is especially so in light of the aging of America. In 1900, there were ten times as many children below 18 as there were adults over 65. By 2030, there will be slightly more people over 65 than under 18.

More than three decades of contraception and abortion have left the United States with a diminished pool of workers to support the elderly, sick, and disabled. If, through contraception, man makes himself the arbiter of when life begins, he will predictably make himself the arbiter, through abortion, suicide, and euthanasia, of when it ends. All are based on a utilitarian approach.

The Supreme Court should have drawn the line in *Cruzan* to affirm that the state may not constitutionally allow the intentional killing of the innocent. And the states should now forbid assisted suicide. But the technological privatization of euthanasia has moved the problem beyond the effective reach of the law. The solution, Pope John Paul II states in *Evangelium Vitae*, must be to restore the conviction that "God . . . is the sole Lord of this life: man cannot do with it as he wills."

| *"The practice of administering a lethal dose to a patient is explicitly repudiated by the Hippocratic Oath, the foundation of medical practice in Western civilization."*

Physicians Should Not Be Allowed to Prescribe Lethal Doses to Terminally Ill Patients

Tom A. Coburn

The Lethal Drug Abuse Prevention Act, introduced as a congressional bill in 1998, would ban the prescribing of lethal narcotics for the purpose of physician-assisted suicide. This proposed federal law, if passed, would override states laws, such as Oregon's, that permit physician-assisted suicide. As of 2000, such legislation had not passed. In the following viewpoint, Oklahoma congressional representative Tom A. Coburn argues in favor of this law. He contends that allowing doctors to prescribe drugs with the intent of killing undermines the medical goal of healing and preserving life. Such a practice also wrongly pressures the severely ill to consent to assisted suicide for the convenience of others, maintains Coburn.

As you read, consider the following questions:

1. What is the purpose of the 1980s Controlled Substances Act, according to Coburn?
2. What is the American Medical Association's stand on physician-assisted suicide?
3. In the author's opinion, why did Oregon voters choose to legalize physician-assisted suicide?

Excerpted from Tom A. Coburn, congressional testimony, House of Representatives on the Lethal Drug Abuse Prevention Act of 1998, 105th Congress, 2nd Session, July 14, 1998.

The genesis of this legislation [to prevent the abuse of lethal drugs] clearly lies in the unfortunate decision of a majority of the voters in the 1997 referendum in the State of Oregon to authorize the practice of so-called "physician-assisted suicide." In doing so, they legally extended to physicians a right to administer to certain patients lethal doses of drugs with the specific intention of ending the patient's life.

Ordinarily, I am very reluctant to contradict the expressed will of a majority of voters in any jurisdiction on any subject. Our entire system of government rests on the principle of the sovereignty of the people and on a trust that, in the long run and most of the time, the people will do the right thing. I believe that. But sometimes the voters can be wrong. And on some occasions when voters make mistakes, they jeopardize the rights of the larger community, and especially those who are most vulnerable. This, I fear, is what the voters in Oregon did in 1997.

If physician-assisted suicide is unleashed in Oregon, it will become extremely dangerous for a person to become seriously ill in that state. The human person is rarely more vulnerable than when gravely ill and confronted with the likelihood of not recovering. For patients who carry that burden, the legalization of physician-assisted suicide adds a new and powerful pressure to allow themselves to be killed. We have seen how, in the Netherlands, a similar policy has led to the elimination of many medically vulnerable patients for the convenience of others.

Physician-assisted suicide is not simply a local Oregon issue. To establish, in even one state, a policy under which the medically vulnerable may be directly killed cheapens life and degrades the medical profession throughout our culture. There are some evils which, perhaps, can be tolerated as long as they are confined to certain localities, but there are others that cannot be allowed to exist at all without poisoning an entire society. Slavery was one such evil; euthanasia is another.

Indeed, the corruption of standards that inevitably accompanies the legalization of physician-assisted suicide is apparent from the chain of circumstances that led to the introduction of the legislation before us today.

The Controlled Substances Act

On the day after the election in 1997, the Drug Enforcement Administration (DEA), in response to inquiries by Representative Henry Hyde and Senator Orrin Hatch, chairmen, respectively, of the House and Senate Judiciary Committees, stated that regardless of the Oregon law, physician-assisted suicide involving lethal doses of controlled substances was a violation of the Controlled Substances Act. Under that Act doctors are licensed to prescribe for their patients drugs that are legal for medical purposes, but not generally available to the public. Those drugs are not banned because they do have great value, when used properly, in controlling or curing illnesses and restoring a patient's health. But they are controlled precisely because, if used improperly, they have the potential for harm, injuring or even, in some cases, killing those to whom they are given. It is the responsibility of physicians to see to it that these drugs are used only for the good of their patients—for "legitimate medical purposes," as the law puts it—but the law also, quite properly, gives doctors wide latitude in applying their own knowledge and experience in the proper use of these substances. It is not a case of the government trying to practice medicine, but rather of the government overseeing the practice of medicine in a way that protects the health and safety of the public.

Preventing the abuse of these drugs in a way that could lead to the death of a patient was very clearly part of the intent of Congress in adopting the Controlled Substances Act. Testifying on behalf of that legislation in 1984, members of Congress noted that the abuse of legal drugs was responsible for a substantial majority of the drug-related deaths at that time, and this was precisely one of the risks against which they intended to protect the public. Congress intended to prevent the abuse of drugs not only on account of their potential "stimulant, depressant, or hallucinogenic" effects, but also, and more urgently, on account of their potential lethal effects. The DEA Administrator, therefore, was absolutely correct when he told Chairman Hyde and Senator Hatch that the practices authorized by Oregon's assisted suicide law would violate the Controlled Substances Act.

But his superior was apparently not so certain. A question

arose about whether the Attorney General would enforce the federal law restricting controlled substances to "legitimate medical purposes." I joined with a number of my congressional colleagues in writing to Attorney General Janet Reno, expressing our view that the federal law was applicable to this situation and needed to be enforced. But on June 5 of 1998 she announced that she did not consider the Controlled Substances Act applicable. Hence, the need for the legislation before us, to correct an error of interpretation by the Attorney General.

Is Killing a "Legitimate Medical Purpose"?

The Attorney General is too good a lawyer to imagine that the meaning of a federal statute can vary from state to state, or can be determined by the law of a single state that contradicts those of all the other states. She knows that the Supremacy Clause in the U.S. Constitution makes laws enacted by Congress the "supreme law of the land," outweighing any state laws that contradict them. Therefore, it must be the belief of the Attorney General that the term "legitimate medical purpose" in federal law includes the practice of administering a lethal dose to a patient. And to this point I must speak not only as a legislator, but as a doctor.

I am . . . a practicing physician and I believe I am competent to address the question of what constitutes a "legitimate medical purpose." And I would note, to begin with, that the practice of administering a lethal dose to a patient is explicitly repudiated by the Hippocratic Oath, the foundation of medical practice in Western civilization. I find it hard to imagine that a practice that for twenty-five centuries doctors swore they would never commit, can suddenly become a "legitimate medical purpose" in federal law because of a referendum in a single state. Since the time of the ancient Greeks, "legitimate medical purposes" have included only measures intended to save and protect life, not to cause death.

The medical profession still overwhelmingly supports the principles of good medical practice enunciated in the Hippocratic Oath. In confidential surveys, only a tiny fraction of practicing physicians say they would be willing to cooperate in taking the life of a suicidal patient. And I am very proud

Threatening Public Health

The use of controlled substances for doctor-assisted suicides would threaten the public health and safety in many ways, including: allowing states and insurance companies to save millions of dollars by offering patients doctor-assisted suicide instead of medical care; stigmatizing and discriminating against the seriously, perhaps terminally ill; and shrouding this one lethal procedure in an impenetrable cloak of secrecy. . . .

Because all human life is inherently valuable, physicians prescribe medicines to heal illness, prolong life, and alleviate suffering. Assisted suicide does not alleviate suffering; it eliminates the sufferer. Neither does it heal illness nor prolong life. Physicians for Compassionate Care agrees with the American Medical Association that "Physician-assisted suicide is fundamentally incompatible with the physician's role as healer, would be difficult or impossible to control, and would pose serious societal risks."

N. Gregory Hamilton, testimony before the House of Representatives, July 14, 1998.

---

that the American Medical Association has not only taken a stand against the practice of "assisted suicide," but has launched an extensive national campaign to educate doctors on pain management. Remarkable new advances have taken place in pain control, and it is now the case that no patient need suffer pain. Many people, including even some doctors, imagine that the only choice for the gravely ill is either to suffer excruciating pain for their remaining days or to end their lives intentionally. This is perhaps the single greatest fear people have about the end of life and it is a major argument used in support of physician-assisted suicide. Yet this argument is technologically obsolete. Medical advances have made it possible for the dying to end their lives in genuine dignity, not wracked with agony but in relative comfort and with a clear mind.

A Tragic Mistake

I am convinced that if the voters in Oregon had known the truth about contemporary medicine, and had not been frightened by the terrible images of end-of-life pain, they would never have made the mistake of authorizing "assisted suicide." I hope that the American Medical Association's campaign to educate physicians about the new advances in pain management are successful enough to free people of the fears that led them to make such a tragic mistake.

Yet at the same time, I am mystified that this same American Medical Association that has done so much to fight against physician-assisted suicide—a practice that will inevitably degrade the medical profession and erode the trust people feel for their doctors—is opposing the legislation before us today. This attitude seems inexplicable. The apparent reason is that the Association seems to see some disadvantage in making doctors liable for violating their professional responsibilities. I think they fail to realize that this legislation before us does not impose new responsibilities on doctors or expose them to new liabilities. It simply reemphasizes the point that killing a patient is not a legitimate medical purpose, a point that has been taken for granted by practicing physicians, the AMA itself, the DEA Administrator, and just about every other authority, with the regrettable exception of Attorney General Reno.

The other concern I have heard expressed about this legislation is that it might expose a doctor to the penalty of losing his federal license to prescribe medicine when, in good faith, he or she gives a patient pain medication that has a side effect of hastening the patient's death. Yet it is very clear from the careful drafting of this bill, using language that the AMA itself recommended in another context, that this danger is purely imaginary. Easing pain is a "legitimate medical purpose," and is clearly differentiated from the direct intention of ending a patient's life. And the Oregon law itself requires a physician to declare in writing the intention to end a life. If a physician complies with the Oregon law, there is no ambiguity about his intention. He would be required to sign a document stating that he is administering a lethal dose pursuant to the patient's request. Doctors who use drugs for pain management do not fill out such a form and evince no such lethal intention.

"Congress is putting at risk the practice of medicine, the treatment of pain and care for the terminally ill."

Potentially Lethal Drugs Are Necessary to Control the Pain Associated with Terminal Illness

John A. Kitzhaber

In the following viewpoint, John A. Kitzhaber argues against a 1999 congressional bill that would outlaw the use of controlled substances for doctor-assisted suicide. If such a bill becomes law, Kitzhaber maintains, physicians will be less likely to administer adequate amounts of the drugs that can curb the pain of the terminally ill. Since higher doses of these drugs can result in unintentional deaths, many doctors fear they might face prosecution if patients under their care die after taking prescribed narcotics. Such fear on the part of physicians could result in the undertreatment of pain for dying patients. Kitzhaber, a medical doctor, is governor of Oregon.

As you read, consider the following questions:
1. What safeguards are written into Oregon's Death with Dignity Act, according to Kitzhaber?
2. In 1998, how many people chose to end their lives under the Death with Dignity Act?
3. In the author's opinion, what is hypocritical about HR 2260?

Reprinted from John A. Kitzhaber, "Congress's Medical Meddlers," *Washington Post National Weekly*, November 8, 1999. Reprinted with permission from the author.

O n November 8, 1994, Oregon voters took the unprece-
dented step of approving the Death With Dignity Act,
which grants terminally ill individuals the choice, under very
limited circumstances, of ending their lives. This decision
was reaffirmed by 60 percent of Oregonians in the 1997 general election. Since then, opponents have been battling from
the courtroom to Congress to try to undo their decision.

In the process, opponents, especially in Congress, have
proven themselves willing to conveniently ignore the rights
of states and the wisdom of voters, and also to disregard the
sanctity of the doctor-patient relationship. Most galling,
however, is the fact that this Congress is more interested in
taking away choices from the terminally ill than in helping
provide health care to the more than 43 million uninsured
Americans—many of whom will die preventable deaths.

Outrageous Claims About Death with Dignity

During both the 1994 and 1997 campaigns, opponents of
the Death With Dignity Act made outrageous claims about
how it would be used. Those fears ranged from a flood of
terminally ill people moving to Oregon to take advantage of
the option to end their own lives, to families conspiring to
end the lives of ill relatives who had become burdens.

These arguments had more to do with unreasoned fear
than they did with facts. The facts of what the law does and
how it has been used in its first year make clear that such
nonsense cannot and has not occurred.

The physician "aid" involves writing a prescription for a
fatal dose of barbiturates, which is self-administered by the
terminally ill individual. To be eligible an individual must
have a terminal illness and be within six months of death.
This diagnosis and prognosis must be concurred upon by
two independent physicians. Either physician can refer the
individual to a psychiatrist for a mental health evaluation if
there is any question about whether the patient is mentally
competent to make the decision.There are other safeguards
such as a waiting period of 15 days between becoming eligible and actually receiving the prescription.

As a consequence, in the first year under the act, only 15
people chose to end their own lives. To put this into per-

The Problem of Unrelieved Pain

Unrelieved pain is a public health crisis in this country. And I am not exaggerating. A consensus statement from the National Cancer Institute workshop on cancer pain indicated that, "undertreatment of pain and other symptoms of cancer is a serious and neglected public health problem." A recent study that was alluded to by the woman in the first panel reported that 26 percent of nursing home residents who were cancer patients received zero pain medication, and they were all in pain.

The pain in our patients, when we service in the hospices, is substantial. For substantial chronic pain the medications of choice are opioids and other narcotics, drugs classified as controlled substances by the Drug Enforcement Administration. The Lethal Drug Abuse Prevention Act will directly affect and unquestionably hinder access to these best treatments that we have available. The problem of unrelieved pain is complex, and there's a number of factors involved. One of the most important factors is the current regulatory environment.

The use of controlled substances is already closely monitored by the DEA and the states. And this monitoring is appropriate in many situations, but it also creates substantial barriers to patient care. Health care professionals fear review and possibly disciplinary action from . . . the DEA. In a survey conducted by New York's public health council, 71 percent of the responding physicians reported they do not prescribe effective medication for cancer pain if such prescriptions would require them to use a special statement monitored prescription form for controlled substances. Seventy-one percent!

Calvin H. Knowlton, testimony before the House of Representatives, July 14, 1998.

---

spective, in 1998 there were 29,314 deaths in Oregon from all causes. Thus, only five of every 10,000 deaths in the state occurred as a result of this new law. Not one of the horror stories predicted by opponents has occurred.

A Dishonest Bill

Yet in October 1999 the House of Representatives substituted its judgment for that of the citizens of Oregon by passing HR 2260, which effectively blocks the implementation of Oregon's law without actually overturning it. For a conservative Congress that prides itself on limited government, on freedom from government intervention, and on privacy and individual liberty, this is a tremendously hypocritical act. Even more hypocritical is the fact that HR 2260 does not directly address the issue of physician aid in dying. Rather, it seeks to prevent the use of controlled substances such as barbiturates in implementing the act. This is disingenuous at best and dishonest at worst. Whether physician aid in dying is an option that should be legal in this country is a legitimate question over which reasonable people can disagree. That is not the question that this Congress is debating.

In its zealous effort to block Oregon's law, Congress has passed a bill that would have a chilling effect on the use of controlled substances in palliative care for the terminally ill. It does this by making it illegal for physicians to knowingly prescribe drugs in order to aid in a death.

This creates a problem, because every day in the legitimate and accepted treatment of terminally ill patients, physicians prescribe controlled substances in dosages that will hasten death. Faced with the specter of investigation by the Drug Enforcement Administration (DEA), prison or loss of their practice, many doctors will treat pain less aggressively than is required for full relief, in order to defend themselves.

Second-Guessing Doctors' Intentions

HR 2260 empowers nameless, unaccountable bureaucrats within the DEA to second-guess the intention of every physician in America. Thus, whenever physicians prescribed narcotics for palliative care, they would be at risk of losing their licenses under this bill. To prevent a choice for Oregon's terminally ill—a choice thoroughly debated and approved by Oregon voters in two general elections—Congress is putting at risk the practice of medicine, the treatment of pain and care for the terminally ill.

How much easier it is to grandstand on this emotional issue than to come to grips with America's true health crisis: the millions who are uninsured. As a physician and as a governor, I urge Congress to focus on this real crisis. Leave Oregonians alone to exercise the individual choice between life and death that they have wisely granted to themselves.

"It is sometimes permissible for us to intend death in order to stop pain."

Euthanasia Is Morally Permissible

Frances M. Kamm

Voluntary euthanasia—the act of killing dying patients with their consent—and physician-assisted suicide are morally permissible, asserts Frances M. Kamm in the following viewpoint. Physicians often participate in a "lesser evil," such as a leg amputation, to bring about a "greater good"—saving a patient's life. In terminal cases involving intractable pain, Kamm argues, pain relief may be the greater good and loss of life the lesser evil. Therefore, she concludes, intentionally killing a dying patient is morally permissible if the patient consents and if death is the only way to stop the pain. Kamm is a New York University philosophy professor who specializes in legal and medical ethics.

As you read, consider the following questions:
1. According to Kamm, in what case may a shorter life be a better life?
2. What is the doctrine of double effect, according to the author?
3. In Kamm's opinion, when might doctors have a duty to kill their patients?

Excerpted from Frances M. Kamm, "A Right to Choose Death?" *Boston Review*, 1997. Reprinted with permission from the author.

D o people have a right to choose death? More particu-larly, are *euthanasia* and *physician-assisted suicide* morally permissible? To clarify terms: Euthanasia involves a death that is intended to benefit the person who dies, and requires a final act by some other person (for example, a doctor); physician-assisted suicide, which requires a final act by the patient, can also be undertaken for the good of that patient, and I will confine my attention to cases in which it is. The essential point is that both involve *intentionally* ending a hu-man life: In voluntary euthanasia, the patient and doctor both intend the death; in physician-assisted suicide, the pa-tient intends the death and the doctor may. But how, some ask, can we ever permit people to intentionally end human lives (even their own lives) without degrading human life? How, others ask, can we simply prevent people from decid-ing when to end their own lives without denying people the autonomy so essential to the value of a human life? As this pair of questions suggests, the debate about the right to choose death may appear to present a stand-off between people who endorse life's intrinsic value, and those who think life's value depends on the interests, judgments, and choices of the person whose life it is.

This picture of irreconcilable moral conflict is, I believe, too despairing about the powers of moral argument. To make headway, however, we may need to pay closer attention to the complexities of cases and the specific moral terrain they oc-cupy: to think about people on medication, being treated by physicians, sometimes relying on technical means to stay alive, trying to decide how to live out what remains of their lives. I will explore this terrain in *moral*, not legal, terms: I will be asking you to consult your moral judgments about cases, and follow out the implications of those judgments. Though this moral argument bears on constitutional argument and on appropriate legislation, I will not propose laws or rules for judges, doctors, or hospital administrators to consult, or worry about slippery slopes created by legally hard cases. The moral landscape affords firmer footing, and does not, I will suggest, permit a blanket ban on euthanasia and physician-assisted suicide: Though both involve intentionally ending human lives, both are sometimes morally permissible. . . .

Logical Troubles?

Before getting to the issue of moral permissibility, we need to overcome a preliminary hurdle. I said that euthanasia and physician-assisted suicide are intended to benefit the patient. Some may object that these ideas make no sense. How is it possible for death to benefit the person who dies? Death eliminates the person—how can we produce a benefit if we eliminate the potential beneficiary?

To see how, consider the parallel question about death as a harm: Can a person be harmed by her own death even though death means that she is no longer around to suffer the harm? Suppose Schubert's life would have included even greater musical achievement had he not died so young. Because musical achievement is an important good, Schubert had a less good life overall than he would have had if he lived longer. But living a less good life is a harm. By excluding those achievements, then, Schubert's death harmed him: it prevented the better life. Now come back to the original concern about how death might be a benefit. Suppose a person's life would go on containing only misery and pain with no compensating goods. That person will be better off living a shorter life containing fewer such uncompensated-for bad things rather than a longer one containing more of them. But living a better life is a benefit. By interfering with the important bads, the person's death benefits him: it prevents the worse life.

It is possible, in short, to benefit a person by ending his life. The concept of euthanasia is, therefore, at least not simply logically confused; similarly for the idea that physician-assisted suicide may be aimed at the good of the patient. But conceptual coherence does not imply moral permissibility. So let's turn now to the moral question: Is it ever morally permissible to benefit a person by hastening his death, even when he requests it?

The Doctrine of Double Effect

Suppose a doctor is treating a terminally ill patient in severe pain. Suppose, too, that the pain can only be managed with morphine, but that giving the morphine is certain to hasten the patient's death. With the patient's consent, the doctor may nevertheless give the morphine. Why so? Because, in this particular case, the greater good for the patient is relief of pain, and the lesser evil is loss of life: after all, the patient is terminally ill, and in severe pain, so life would end soon anyway and is not of very good quality. So the patient is overall benefited by having a shorter pain-free life rather than a longer, even more painful life. (Notice that this could be true even if the morphine put the patient in a deep unconscious state from which he never awoke, so that he never consciously experienced pain-free time.)

Serving the Interests of the Patient

We should not permit our hubris of thinking we can overcome the suffering of dying to keep the physician from acceding to the patient's request for a lethal dose. We hear misguided claims that following the Hippocratic Oath would keep physicians from assisting in suicide. The spirit of the Hippocratic Oath says the physician should be devoted to the patient's interests. How we define those interests today should not be limited by our understanding of medicine over two millennia ago.

Arthur Rifkin, *Friends Journal*, October 1997.

In giving morphine to produce pain relief, the doctor foresees with certainty (let's assume) that the patient will die soon. Still, death is a side-effect of the medication, not the doctor's goal or reason for giving it: the doctor, that is, is not *intending* the patient's death, and would give the medication even if he thought death would not result. (If I have a drink to soothe my nerves and foresee a hangover, it does not follow that I intend the hangover.) Because the intended death is not present, we don't yet have a case of euthanasia or physician-assisted suicide. At the same time, in giving morphine for pain relief, the doctor is not simply letting the patient die as the disease runs its course; he administers a drug which causes death. So I think this should be understood as a case of killing, even though the doctor does not intend the death. (In other cases we have no trouble seeing that it is possible to kill without intending death: consider a driver who runs someone over while speeding.)

Now suppose the morphine loses its power to reduce the

intensity of the patient's pain, but that administering it would still shorten the patient's life and thus limit the duration of his pain. Suppose, too, that the patient requests the morphine; fully aware of its effects, he wants to take it so that it will end his pain by killing him. In short, we now have a case of *morphine for death* rather than *morphine for pain relief*. Is it still morally permissible to give the morphine? Some people say that we may not kill in this case. They do not deny that relief of pain is still the greater good and death the lesser evil: they know that the consequences are essentially the same as in the case of morphine for pain relief. The problem, they say, lies in a difference of intent. In the case of giving morphine for pain relief, we intend the pain relief, and merely foresee the death; but in the case of giving morphine for death, we intend the death (which is the lesser evil): we would not give the morphine if we did not expect the death. But some people think it is impermissible to act with the intent to produce an evil. They support what is called the *doctrine of double effect*, according to which there is a large moral difference between acting with the foresight that one's conduct will have some evil consequence and acting with the intent to produce that same evil (even as part of or means to a greater good). So whereas killing the patient by giving morphine for pain relief is permissible, killing the patient by giving morphine for death is impermissible.

The Greater Good

The distinction between intending an evil and merely foreseeing it sometimes makes a moral difference. But does it provide a reason to refrain from performing euthanasia or assisting in suicide? I think not. On many occasions already, doctors (with a patient's consent) *intend the lesser evil* to a person in order *to produce his own greater good*. For example, a doctor may intentionally amputate a healthy leg (the lesser evil) in order to get at and remove a cancerous tumor, thereby saving the patient's life (the greater good). Or, he may intentionally cause blindness in a patient if seeing would somehow, for example, destroy the patient's brain, or cause him to die. Furthermore, he may intentionally cause someone pain, thereby acting contrary to a duty to relieve suffering, if this helps to save the person's life. The duty to save life sometimes just outweighs the other duty. Why then is it impermissible for doctors to intend death when it is the lesser evil, in order to produce the greater good of no pain; why is it morally wrong to benefit the patient by giving her a shorter, less painful life rather than having her endure a longer, more painful one? Recall that in the case of morphine for pain relief, it was assumed that death would be the lesser evil and pain relief the greater good. That was one reason we could give the morphine. Why is it wrong, then, for doctors sometimes to act against a duty to preserve life in order to relieve pain, just as they could sometimes act against a duty not to intend pain in order to save a life?

To summarize, I have constructed a three-step argument for physician-assisted suicide and euthanasia. Assuming patient consent:

1. We may permissibly cause death as a side effect if it relieves pain, because sometimes death is a lesser evil and pain relief a greater good.
2. We may permissibly intend other lesser evils to the patient, for the sake of her greater good.
3. Therefore, when death is a lesser evil, it is sometimes permissible for us to intend death in order to stop pain.

Thus, suppose we accept that it is sometimes permissible to *knowingly* shorten a life by giving pain-relieving medication, and agree, too, that it is sometimes permissible for a doctor to *intend* a lesser evil in order to produce a greater good. How, then, can it be wrong to *intentionally* shorten a life when that will produce the greater good? . . .

An Argument for Duty

According to the three-step argument, a doctor is *permitted* to give morphine for pain relief, even though he knows it will expedite the patient's death, if death is the lesser evil. But I think we can say more. Suppose, as I have stipulated, that giving morphine is the only way for a doctor to relieve a patient's suffering. A doctor, I assume, has a duty to relieve suffering. I conclude that the doctor has a *duty* to relieve suffering by giving the morphine, if the patient requests this. He cannot refuse to give the morphine on the ground that he will be a killer if he does.

If doctors have a duty to relieve pain, and even being a killer does not override this duty when the patient requests morphine for pain relief, then perhaps they also have a duty, not merely a permission, to kill their patients, or aid in their being killed, intending their deaths in order to relieve suffering. Now we have a new argument. Assuming patient consent:

1. There is sometimes a duty to treat pain even if it foreseeably makes one a killer, when death is the lesser evil and no pain is the greater good.
2. There is a duty to intend the other lesser evils (e.g., amputation) for a patient's own greater good.
3. There is sometimes a duty to kill the patient, or assist in his being killed, intending his death when this is the lesser evil and pain relief the greater good.

| *"Killing, even for the best reasons, has generally been seen by physicians as unprofessional and immoral."*

Physicians Should Not Be Allowed to Participate in Euthanasia

Alan B. Astrow

Physicians should not be allowed to honor requests for assisted suicide and euthanasia, contends Alan B. Astrow in the following viewpoint. Granting doctors a "license to kill" would contradict the life-serving purposes of medicine and ultimately create more difficult conflicts for the terminally ill and their loved ones. Instead of endorsing euthanasia, Astrow argues, medical policymakers should see that doctors and nurses acquire better training in pain alleviation and comfort care for the dying. Astrow, a medical doctor, is the program director in hematology and oncology at St. Vincent's Hospital and Medical Center of New York.

As you read, consider the following questions:

1. According to Astrow, what two problems are central to the medical profession's treatment of the dying?
2. How would professionally supervised suicide affect public morale, in the author's opinion?
3. What experience strengthened Astrow's recognition that doctors often do not know how to discuss serious illnesses with their patients?

Excerpted from Alan B. Astrow, *Facing Death: Where Culture, Religion, and Medicine Meet.* Reprinted with permission from Yale University Press.

As I write this, a second cousin, aged eighty-two, lies comatose on a ventilator in the intensive care unit of a large public hospital in New York City. He had had a mild stroke and then was suddenly stricken three weeks ago with what appears to have been a brain stem stroke. While now unresponsive to all stimuli, he still has minimal activity on a brain scan and so has not met the criteria for brain death. His physicians believe that the likelihood for recovery is near zero, but because he has never explicitly stated his wishes regarding how he would want to be treated in such circumstances they will not remove him from the ventilator. (His closest relative would consent to removal.) He is now also on tube feedings and on intravenously administered antibiotics for pneumonia.

My cousin's fate, suspended between life and death, captures for me the missing dimension to discussions about assisted suicide and euthanasia. Although these topics arouse strong emotions, I see them as peripheral to the care of most dying patients. As a practicing oncologist and hematologist, I have cared for many patients dying from cancer. Legalization of assisted suicide and euthanasia would do little, in my view, to enhance the comfort of these patients and would threaten substantial public harm and damage to the morale of the profession. I see instead two central problems in our treatment of the chronically ill and dying: (1) the failure to acknowledge that the patient is dying and that comfort is the most appropriate goal, and (2) the misuse of high technology in a manner that prolongs the dying process.

My cousin does not require a statute legalizing euthanasia to be allowed to die in peace. He only requires that our profession and our health care institutions resolve to withdraw intrusive medical technology with the family's consent when that technology serves no human purpose. I serve on the staff of a Catholic hospital where, accompanying a tradition of hostility to active life-taking, a strong aversion to the delivery of futile or nonbeneficial care usually leads to the withdrawal of ventilatory support in cases like that of my cousin. I suspect that there is considerable public confusion in this area, that an outlook that holds life sacred is mistakenly seen as requiring endless life support.

In my own field of medical oncology, one frequently encounters the related problem of aggressive treatment continued past any realistic hope of benefit. Dying patients are sometimes identified with their tumors, and continued "attacks" by chemotherapy and radiation therapy may prolong rather than relieve their suffering. I agree with bioethicist Daniel Callahan that it is precisely the "obeisance to medical technology" that has led to the fear of a "technologically induced bad death" and spurred public support for physician-assisted suicide. Doctors and patients together need to face our finitude openly and acknowledge the limits to curative medical interventions. Suffering and death are parts of life that we rightly struggle against but ultimately have to accept. Angry disillusionment may follow an overly optimistic assessment of modern medicine's power. As a result, our approach to incurable illness may focus unnecessarily on the extremes of treatment without limit and at all cost or, alternatively, a swift clinical end. Expanded access to hospice services and improved training of doctors and nurses in comfort care for the dying might reassure patients and their families that they need not confront chronic progressive illness alone.

Euthanasia Is Not the Answer

The argument for physician-assisted suicide and euthanasia rests on those cases of chronically ill patients who can find comfort nowhere but in death. As an oncologist I too have treated many patients whose uncontrolled tumors have produced intractable pain, profound nausea and anorexia, foul-smelling discharges, and worse, for whom death could be seen only as a blessing. In most instances, though, a withdrawal of active medical treatment combined with unstinting use of analgesics and sedatives to control symptoms allows the patient to die comfortably and peacefully. Western religious traditions acknowledge the principle of "double effect": treatment intended to relieve the suffering of a person with advanced incurable disease is morally acceptable even if that treatment secondarily shortens the person's life. There is an inherent ambiguity in the care of the dying, and the line between relief of suffering and end of life is often blurred. I wonder at times whether most physicians understand that providing adequate doses of morphine to control pain and suffering for a dying patient is not considered "killing" but instead represents symptom relief within the best traditions of medicine.

I have certainly treated patients who, it seemed, died "too slowly" despite my efforts to provide for their comfort. One such patient with head and neck cancer and advanced liver metastases wasted away over a three-week period while on a morphine drip, to the great distress of his family. A nurse who knew the patient but had not been directly involved in caring for him later told me that had we been more attentive to his grimaces we might have increased the rate of his morphine drip more quickly. This sort of teamwork offers the best hope for relief of suffering in dying patients. Team members can work closely with the patient and family to forestall conflicts, avoid moral crises, and share the emotional burden that these inherently troubling situations carry.

Some patients who are depressed and discouraged by the prospect of lingering physical decline but are not yet "actively dying" want an end to their suffering and assistance in ending their lives. I think here of some patients with Lou Gehrig's disease (ALS), Alzheimer's, stroke syndromes, or AIDS. We can all understand these wishes; none of us can be sure how we might respond to such grim prospects. At the risk of sounding callous, nevertheless, I believe that physicians should not honor such requests. While we are obliged to respect the desires of patient and family, the choice of death over life cannot be viewed as just another choice if medicine is to maintain its moral stature. The patient's prerogative must be exercised within the framework of generally accepted standards of physician conduct. Killing, even for the best reasons, has generally been seen by physicians as unprofessional and immoral. Most physicians, aware of the uncertainties of medical decision-making, the strain of caring for the chronically ill, and the hostile feelings that such patients may engender, understand the need to accept limits to what a physician is empowered to do. I agree with Leon Kass: were physicians to attack life directly, we would "contradict the inner meaning of our own profession." To put physicians in the role of judging the appropriateness of a person's request to end his life can only further "medicalize" a fundamental life experience whose meaning has already been diminished by the dominance of medical technology.

The Public Morale

We need to consider the impact of legally sanctioned and professionally monitored suicide on the public morale as well. Persons who wish to end their lives can usually find the means to do so. In facilitating that choice by granting professionals a license to kill, however, we all become complicit in an antisocial act. The reduction of end-of-life decision-making to a matter of private choice threatens to reinforce the isolation of the chronically ill and their families. How we die carries with it a profound meaning not only for the dying person, but also for all those who have loved and cared for that person. Often, suicide provides only the illusion of a solution to the fundamental human problems of disappointment, suffering, and death and simply transfers the burdens and conflicts at the end of life to the loved ones left behind.

The stricture against active life-taking carries with it a communal obligation to support those suffering from serious illness. Sickness and death should serve as constant reminders of our common bonds and need for one another. A seriously ill and disheartened person may overcome despair and rediscover meaning and purpose in life. We need to encourage those efforts on a personal level by not turning away from people with incurable illness and on a social level by helping them continue to work and maintain their positions within their communities. We also need to assure the incurably ill that, when all else fails, we will provide for their comfort.

In persons with end-stage ALS, for instance (at substantial risk, say, of choking on their own saliva), I would think it medically and morally proper for a physician familiar with the patient to provide morphine for comfort. In contrast, I believe that to have euthanized that same person, even with the person's consent, six months earlier in the course of the illness—or for a stranger with an M.D. to poison that person with carbon monoxide—would be murder. . . .

Realistic Hope

An honest appraisal of what medicine can and cannot do will be central to any efforts to improve care of the dying. In the field of cancer treatment, for example, despite all the genuine advances and the promise for the future, large numbers of our patients die and will continue to die of their disease. Sherwin Nuland has protested movingly against giving false hope to cancer patients and their families. "I never had a single experience in which an oncology consultation did not result in a recommendation to treat," he wrote in *How We Die.*

While Nuland overstates the case—in my experience many, if not most, oncologists are honest and caring physicians—his broader point has merit. The field as a whole has been advertised in a way that creates unrealistic expectations in the public's mind. We have made giant strides in earlier and more accurate diagnosis of cancer and in our understanding of the molecular mechanisms of oncogenesis and metastasis, and we have also achieved striking success in treating several of the less common malignancies such as Hodgkin's disease and the non-Hodgkin's lymphomas, childhood leukemia, and testicular cancer. Nevertheless the outlook for the vast majority of cancer patients has changed little over the past sixty years. In 1990, half a million Americans died of cancer, 23 percent of all deaths.

The sad contrast between the promise of our contemporary scientific approach to cancer treatment and the reality of unhappy outcomes in so many of our cancer patients promotes misunderstanding, catastrophic disappointment, and anger. Patients are often sent to medical oncologists when surgeons and radiation therapists have exhausted all other options. The patients come with the hope that we will enable them to live, not help them to die. Often the referring doctors create false expectations to relieve their own burden of guilt. Or they might rid themselves of an "unsuccessful case" by delivering a harsh prognosis, leaving the patient emotionally devastated. The setting of achievable goals is undermined, and open engagement with patient and family becomes a lonely and draining pursuit. In the absence of effective support, the patient with progressive incurable cancer may be subtly encouraged simply to end it all.

Let me illustrate. A woman in her sixties was referred to me by an internist colleague. She had complained only of a cough, but after diagnostic evaluation an unresectable biliary tract cancer was found. Two days before her first scheduled appointment with me, she saw a well-known surgeon from the cancer center across town who told her that there was nothing that could be done. The woman canceled her appointment with me, and the next day I was told by her internist that she had been found dead in her apartment.

Reprinted by permission of Peter Steiner.

Such experiences have reinforced my conviction that physicians are ill equipped to decide whether a person's life is worth living. The ability to offer realistic hope to a person with a critical illness is a subtle art that not all physicians possess and that even the most skilled have difficulty sustaining. The diagnosis of incurable illness presents the patient with both a physical and a spiritual crisis. People suddenly confront long evaded questions of meaning and purpose. What does it mean to be alive? Why go on in the face of incurable illness? Rather than function as judge and executioner, the physician could serve as a crucial moral presence in this setting, a source of strength and courage.

The Need for Open Discussion

Open discussion of these sorts of existential issues within the profession and amidst the public at large, along with frank acknowledgment of the limits of medical technology, may help us to clarify values, achieve public consensus, and improve the care of the dying. I agree with Christopher Lasch that medicine has ill served the public and itself by focusing excessively on technique. "Like other professions," Lasch has written, "medicine has been uncomfortable with its role in shaping public opinion, preferring to address itself to the technical problems it feels qualified to solve. But its silence on the broad ethical questions that govern popular expectations leads the public to expect far too much of medicine and create painful and now familiar situations in which doctors themselves are expected to decide questions of life and death."

Even as we physicians own up to our shortcomings in this area, we have reason to be hopeful. There is far less shame and secrecy in the care of cancer patients, for instance, than was the case thirty years ago. The success of Nuland's book testifies to the public's hunger for truthfulness in the care of the dying. . . . The growth of the hospice movement, as well as recent decisions of public figures like Jacqueline Kennedy Onassis, who chose to die at home, and Richard Nixon, who elected to forgo invasive life support, are also encouraging signs of a new public awareness of limits. Even the movement to legalize physician-assisted suicide, while I disagree with its goal, has served to focus public attention on the treatment of the incurably ill. The New York State Task Force on Life and Law has issued a two-hundred-page report on physician-assisted suicide. I suggest that the next step we take should be to move from ethical reflection to an investigation of social reality. Perhaps a national study on the care given to those at the end of life is called for. If we doctors are to eschew suicide as a solution, we will have to understand the true needs of the progressively ill and act, as a profession and as a society, to address them.

Periodical Bibliography

The following articles have been selected to supplement the diverse views presented in this chapter. Addresses are provided for periodicals not indexed in the *Readers' Guide to Periodical Literature*, the *Alternative Press Index*, the *Social Sciences Index*, or the *Index to Legal Periodicals and Books*.

Tom L. Beauchamp — "Refusals of Treatment and Requests for Death," *Kennedy Institute of Ethics Journal*, December 1996. Available from the Johns Hopkins University Press, 2715 N. Charles St., Baltimore, MD 21218-4319.

Neil Campbell — "A Problem for the Idea of Voluntary Euthanasia," *Journal of Medical Ethics*, June 1999. Available from BMJ Publishing Group, PO Box 590A, Kennebunkport, ME 14146.

Anne E. Fade — "Withdrawing Life Support from the Terminally Ill," *USA Today Magazine*, January 1996.

Nancy Harvey — "Dying Like a Dog," *First Things*, April 1995. Available from 156 Fifth Ave., Suite 400, New York, NY 10010.

Jim Holt — "Sunny Side Up," *New Republic*, February 21, 1994.

M. Cathleen Kaveny — "Death Needs No Assistants," *U.S. Catholic*, January 1999.

Diane E. Meier et al. — "A National Survey of Physician-Assisted Suicide and Euthanasia in the United States," *New England Journal of Medicine*, April 23, 1998. Available from 1440 Main St., Waltham, MA 02154-1600.

John J. Paris — "Hugh Finn's 'Right to Die,'" *America*, October 31, 1998.

William E. Phipps — "Defining Death: Ethical, Moral, and Legal Factors," *USA Today Magazine*, January 1996.

Wesley J. Smith — "Suicide Unlimited in Oregon," *Weekly Standard*, November 8, 1999. Available from 1211 Avenue of the Americas, New York, NY 10036.

Daniel P. Sulmasy — "Killing and Allowing to Die: Another Look," *Journal of Law, Medicine, and Ethics*, Spring 1998.

CHAPTER 4

Do the Terminally Ill Have the Right to Die?

Chapter Preface

In 1994, Oregon passed the Death with Dignity Act, which legalized physician-assisted suicide for terminally ill patients within six months of death. The controversial state law went into effect in 1997, after Oregon voters turned down a ballot measure that would have repealed it. Questions raised by Oregon's sanctioning of assisted suicide have provoked fierce debate among lawmakers, ethicists, and the general public.

Supporters of Oregon's Death with Dignity Act maintain that the terminally ill often experience relentless pain and should have the right to kill themselves rather than suffer through the last agonizing weeks of the dying process. Assisted suicide, proponents argue, simply hastens a process that terminal disease has already set in motion, granting the fatally ill a modicum of dignity and control over their final days. Moreover, supporters point out, the Oregon law includes safeguards that prevent potential abuses of doctor-assisted suicide: The individual requesting suicide must be mentally competent, two physicians must agree on a terminal prognosis, a fifteen-day waiting period must pass before the dying person receives the lethal prescription, and the fatal dose must be self-administered.

Critics, however, argue that legalized assisted suicide poses a threat to vulnerable patients who could be pressured by doctors or family members into ending their lives prematurely. Moreover, many medical ethicists contend, the practice of assisted suicide compromises the physician's duty to heal and sustain life. If legalized assisted suicide becomes more common, they warn, it may become difficult to prohibit the spread of the practice to those who are not terminally ill, such as the disabled, the critically injured, or those with chronic but not fatal illnesses. Rather than sanction assisted suicide, critics maintain, the medical community should focus on improving pain relief and comfort care for the severely ill.

Oregon's Death with Dignity Act has set the stage for other states to question their own policies on assisted suicide and end-of-life care. The following chapter presents further debate on this and other issues bearing on a patient's right to die.

> *"Terminal patients may rationally decide that death with dignity in a manner and time of their own choosing is preferable to a slow, agonizing, prolonged death."*

The Terminally Ill Should Have Access to Assisted Suicide

Erdman B. Palmore

In the following viewpoint, Erdman B. Palmore argues that the terminally ill should have the right to choose the time of their death. Dying people may want to commit suicide in order to end their own suffering or to ease the emotional and financial burdens on their loved ones, and Palmore believes their wishes should be respected. He maintains that legalizing physician-assisted suicide would decriminalize an already common procedure and reduce the problems resulting from unsuccessful suicide attempts on the part of the fatally ill. Palmore is a professor emeritus at the Duke University Center for the Study of Aging.

As you read, consider the following questions:
1. According to J. Werth and D.C. Cobia, cited by the author, what three criteria can help determine if a decision to commit suicide is rational?
2. What is Palmore's response to the argument that endorsing suicide for the dying will encourage suicide among the disabled and elderly?
3. In the author's opinion, how could people be protected from physicians who abuse the legal right to assist suicides?

Reprinted from Erdman B. Palmore, "Suicide Can Be Rational for Senescent or Terminal Patients," in *Contemporary Perspectives on Rational Suicide*, edited by James L. Werth Jr. Reprinted with permission from Erdman B. Palmore.

B ecause the concept of "rational suicide" is relatively new (fewer than a couple of decades old), there has been little research and discussion about it either in the mass media or in scholarly books and journals. There has been even less discussion of how it applies to senescent or terminal patients. This viewpoint is an attempt to point out that the arguments for rational suicide apply with particular cogency to senescent or terminal patients, and that arguments against it are especially weak when applied to these patients.

Although I believe that suicide can be rational for adults of all ages, I believe it is most likely to be rational among those with intolerable conditions and short life expectancies because of extreme old age or terminal illness. Recent surveys of professionals and of the public show increasing support for the concept of rational suicide, especially in these cases.

I first define my terms, then present the arguments for rational suicide among senescent and terminal patients, and then refute the arguments against it. At the end I discuss arguments with special relevance to the subordinate issue of physician-assisted suicide.

Definitions

By *suicide* I mean the act of taking one's own life voluntarily and intentionally. This includes physician-assisted suicide but does not include euthanasia, which is the act of killing someone else (in a relatively painless way). Whether euthanasia is ever rational or morally justified is another debate, which should not be confused with the question of rational suicide.

By *rational* I mean based on reason and logic: reasonable. This does not imply that everyone would agree with the reasoning or the decision reached, but that the decision is based on logical reasoning rather than on some emotional impulse or illogical thinking.

I agree with J. Werth and D.C. Cobia's three criteria for judging whether a decision to suicide is rational or not:

1. The person considering suicide has an unremitting hopeless condition, such as terminal illness, severe physical and/or psychological pain, physically or mentally debilitating and/or deteriorating conditions, or quality of life

no longer acceptable to the individual.

2. The person makes the decision as a free choice.

3. The person has engaged in a sound decision-making process including consultation with a mental health professional to assess mental competence (and to exclude treatable depression); a nonimpulsive consideration of all alternatives; consideration of the congruence of the act with one's personal values and of the impact on significant others; and consultation with objective others and with significant others.

By *senescent* I do not mean most people over 65 years of age, because the average 65-year-old can expect another 17 or more years of life, most of which will be active years in reasonably good health. Eighty percent of persons over the age of 65 years are healthy enough to do their normal activities. I am not going to discuss these healthy elders, because I believe age alone is not sufficient to make suicide rational. By *senescent* I mean people of extreme old age with a short life expectancy who have deteriorated so far that they find continued existence worthless or unbearable. Senescent people may not yet be terminal, but they usually die within a few years.

By *terminal patients* I mean patients who are so critically ill that they are expected to die within 6 months.

Arguments for Rational Suicide

They Are Dying Already. This is perhaps the strongest argument for rational suicide among terminal patients. Who can object to ending intractable pain and suffering if the patient is dying already? For terminal patients, the question is not "to be or not to be." They will soon "not be," whether by rational suicide or by painful prolongation of the dying process. In such a case, suicide is simply a speeding up of the dying process that has already begun.

For senescent but not yet terminal patients, the choice may be more difficult because they may have a year or more of life left, and some may choose to endure and "hope against hope" that somehow things will improve. But if they are already invalids, suffering from hopeless diseases such as AIDS, Alzheimer's disease, or terminal cancer, who find their lives miserable and their circumstances intolerable, they may rationally choose to end their misery.

Death With Dignity. After weighing the "costs and benefits," senescent or terminal patients may rationally decide that death with dignity in a manner and time of their own choosing is preferable to a slow, agonizing, prolonged death in which they suffer all the indignities of loss of control and physical and mental function or become a vegetable.

Reducing the Costs and Waste of Expensive Medical Resources. Because most of the costs of terminal care, especially among the very old, are borne by Medicare and Medicaid, rational suicide among these patients could substantially reduce the projected deficit in these programs. Thus suicide among senescent and terminal patients might even be considered a patriotic act!

There is now a federal requirement that all hospitals ask patients upon admission if they have a living will and, if they do not, give them information and forms to sign if they wish. This was prompted by a desire to both increase patients' self-determination and reduce costs of useless treatments.

Many medical professionals, in the absence of a living will or other directives to the contrary, feel obligated to do everything possible to prolong the lives of terminal patients regardless of how hopeless the prognosis or how expensive and painful the treatment. These professionals may cite the Hippocratic Oath or fear of malpractice liability as justification for their actions.

One study found that even if there is a living will or relatives do not want to prolong the dying, many medical professionals ignore these wishes and proceed with expensive and extraordinary treatments. One certain way to prevent this is rational suicide.

Reducing the Emotional and Financial Strain on Family and Friends. Dying patients may rationally decide that the most loving thing they can do for their family and friends is to end, through suicide, the financial strain caused by their nursing care and medication, and the emotional pain resulting from the indignities of the dying process.

Right to Die. Suicide is now legal in all 50 states. The right to die through suicide is as inalienable a right as the right to live. This right is implied by the First Amendment (freedom of religion) and by other amendments that have been interpreted to guarantee the right to do what one wishes with one's own body (as in the right to refuse medical treatment, have an abortion, and so forth). This right becomes even more cogent for those who will soon die because of senescence or terminal illness. . . .

Arguments Against Rational Suicide

Suffering Is Beneficial. This argument asserts that one should not end suffering through suicide because suffering can be beneficial in some strange way, such as by strengthening character, giving one sympathy for others who suffer, giving one a deeper appreciation for the joys of life, and so forth.

This argument sounds particularly hollow if applied to people who are about to die, such as senescent and terminal patients. Although those who have a normal life left may try to make the best of necessary suffering by looking for the "silver lining," it seems heartless to tell dying people that they must not end their misery through suicide because suffering is good for them.

Suicide Is a Result of Mental Illness. This argument simply asserts that by definition no "normal" person would want to commit suicide, that all suicide is the result of depression or some other mental illness, and therefore that suicide can never be rational. A variant of this argument is that suicidal persons have difficulty recognizing or generating alternative solutions to their problems, and therefore suicide is not a rational choice weighed against all possible alternatives.

Although it is true that *some* suicides result from depression or other mental illness, it is also true that many suicides are committed by persons with no signs of any mental illness, who are completely rational in every way, and who give clear and reasonable explanations for their suicide. This is especially true of senescent and terminal patients because their debilitated conditions, pain, and approaching deaths can be reasonable explanations for committing suicide.

Suicide Is Irreversible. This argument says that suicide is not rational because it is irreversible and a rational person might choose to live at some later point in time if the situation improves, or a cure is found, or the person feels better.

Although this argument may have merit for persons with normal life expectancy, it seems weak, if not irrelevant, when applied to persons who are already dying. For terminal patients, by definition, there is no hope that the situation will improve or a cure will be found before the person's death.

The Benefits of Assisted Death

Permitting physician-assisted suicide might have positive effects in addition to minimizing suffering. Some patients facing an irreversible progressive disease take their own lives while they are still in reasonably good health, because they fear that if they wait, they will find themselves unable to do so—either because they are too impaired to act or because they are confined to a hospital. Knowing that assisted death would be available when they needed it would undoubtedly lead many incurably ill people to postpone ending their lives. They would thus live longer and, even more important, they would live in more peace.

Marcia Angell, *Regulating How We Die*, ed. Linda L. Emanuel, 1998.

Pain Can Be Reduced to Tolerable Levels. E. Shneidman argues that suicide is often caused by intolerable pain. He says that with modern drugs and counseling the pain can be reduced or the person's tolerance of pain can be increased so that suicide would no longer be chosen.

Although this is true in some cases, there are also terminal cases in which no amount of drugs, short of enough to cause complete unconsciousness, can control the pain, and no amount of counseling can increase pain tolerance to sufficient levels to prevent the desire for suicide.

Society Loses the Benefits of the Person's Life. This is the social obligation argument that asserts that because everyone has an obligation to contribute whatever they can to others, suicide robs society of the benefits that the person could contribute if he or she continued to live. It is argued that everyone can contribute some skill or special knowledge or at least love as long as they live.

This argument also seems irrelevant to people who are dying and helpless, racked with intolerable pain. Rather than contributing anything to society, they are only draining society's resources. They may rationally decide that the most loving thing they can do for their relatives and friends is to end their strain and upset through suicide. This has been called "altruistic suicide" by sociologist Emil Durkheim.

Acceptance of Rational Suicide Leads to Disorientation and Anxiety. If the concept of rational suicide is generally accepted, some say it would undermine the clear prohibition of suicide and force many people to make the choice between life and death. This would lead to confusion, disorientation, and anxiety as to whether someone has made or is making the right choice.

This argument fails to recognize that, like it or not, suicide is now legal in all 50 states. Therefore many people are already forced to consider that option. Indeed, many philosophers (such as the existentialists) and ethicists argue that the basic question facing everyone all the time is whether to continue living or not. This is especially true for senescent and terminal patients who are facing imminent death.

Acceptance of Rational Suicide May Lead to Some Persons Being Manipulated into Suicide. Margaret Battin has argued that old and terminally ill patients are especially vulnerable to being pressured against their will to commit suicide because they may be made to feel obligated to do so. Some have called this a kind of ageism in which it is assumed that very old people have little value, consume too much medical care, and therefore should be encouraged to end their lives.

Pressuring anyone of any age or condition to commit suicide against her or his will is immoral and almost a contradiction in terms. We have defined suicide as the *voluntary* taking of one's own life. However, to single out the aged and say that theirs can never be a rational suicide is just as much a kind of ageism as is saying that they have an obligation to commit suicide.

On a related topic, healthcare should not be rationed on the basis of old age. If healthcare must be rationed at all, it should be on the basis of efficacy, prognosis, and urgency, not age. If rational suicide for senescent and terminal patients were more widely accepted, it could substantially reduce the pressures to ration healthcare (see the third "pro" argument).

A Slippery Slope?

H.R. Moody worries that the acceptance of suicide as rational "will lead us down the slippery slope" to where it is difficult to draw the line at which it is clear when someone is a candidate for rational suicide. S.G. Post warns that this could result in *all* disabled, elderly, or otherwise dependent persons being labeled as living "meaningless" lives and therefore being encouraged to commit suicide.

This argument is usually the last refuge of the desperate who can find no convincing argument against a specified behavior (suicide for senescent and terminal patients) but attempt to spread the fear that it could lead to other more terrible behaviors. This is like the argument that we should have prohibition against all alcohol because drinking any amount of alcohol may lead to terrible things like alcoholism, drunken driving, murder, and other crimes. Or that dancing can lead to rape. Or that playing cards can lead to gambling and poverty.

Each specified behavior should be judged on its own merit, rather than on fears about what that behavior might sometimes lead to. Therefore, suicide for senescent and terminal patients should be judged on its own merit rather than on fears that it may lead to encouraging suicide among many other persons.

Physician-Assisted Rational Suicide

A subordinate question is whether physicians (or other medical professionals) should be allowed to assist a person to commit rational suicide. If we assume that suicide may be rational in some cases, such as with senescent or terminal patients, then there are several additional arguments to support the legalization of physician assistance.

1. Physicians should have the freedom of conscience to determine if assisted suicide is the most humane treatment available. Restricting physicians' right to relieve pain through assisting in suicide is government interference with medical practice. Physicians may feel an ethical duty

toward their senescent or terminal patients to help them end their suffering.

2. Legalizing physician-assisted suicide would decriminalize a practice that is already widespread. Many physicians will admit that they have assisted in a suicide, or they know of other physicians who have done so, usually through making a lethal dose of drugs available. Even more physicians will progressively increase various drugs in attempts to cover pain, even though these doses hasten death.

3. Physician-assisted suicide would reduce the occurrence of botched attempts at suicide and all the problems resulting from such attempts. Many patients do not fear suicide; they only fear failure of an attempt, which would make their condition even more miserable.

4. Assisting suicide of a senescent or terminal patient is consistent with the Hippocratic Oath to "do no harm." It does not harm a terminal patient to help hasten the dying process; indeed, it may be the only way to help some patients relieve their pain. (See the fifth "con" argument.)

5. Fears that physicians might abuse a legal right to assist in rational suicide could be allayed by establishing various criteria for judging whether a suicide is rational or not (such as in the section on definitions in this viewpoint) and establishing review committees (including psychiatrists to detect temporary depression or other mental illness, social workers to counsel the patient, and so forth), which would rule on the rationality of the request for assistance in suicide.

6. No physician would be forced to assist in suicide. Just as some physicians refuse to perform an abortion because it is contrary to their personal beliefs, physicians could refuse requests to assist in suicide if it is contrary to their beliefs.

Accepting Rational Suicide

Despite the relative recency of the concept, rational suicide for senescent or terminal patients is gaining more and more acceptance among healthcare professionals, ethicists, religious leaders, attorneys, sociologists, and the public at large. There are at least five arguments for rational suicide that are especially cogent if applied to senescent and terminal patients.

The arguments advanced against rational suicide are weak or not applicable to such patients. There are several additional arguments that support the legalization of physician-assisted suicide in such cases.

The wider acceptance of rational suicide among senescent and terminal patients would have many benefits for the suffering patients, their families, the medical professions, and society in general.

"Legalizing assisted suicide for people who are diagnosed with a terminal illness is wrong."

The Terminally Ill Should Not Have Access to Assisted Suicide

Wesley J. Smith

Wesley J. Smith is an attorney for the International Anti-Euthanasia Task Force and the author of *Forced Exit: The Slippery Slope from Assisted Suicide to Legalized Murder*. In the following viewpoint, Smith argues that sanctioning assisted suicide devalues the lives of sick and dying people and undermines a physician's oath to "do no harm." Nurturing and effective pain control should be the preferred treatments for the terminally ill, Smith maintains. If the legalization of assisted suicide spreads, he warns, the nonfatally ill and the disabled will face increased pressure to end their lives in order to cut health-care costs.

As you read, consider the following questions:
1. According to Smith, which groups have formed a coalition to oppose assisted suicide?
2. Why have many people supported the legalization of assisted suicide, in the author's opinion?
3. What is the principle of double-effect, according to Smith?

Excerpted from Wesley J. Smith, "When Death Is Our Physician," *New Oxford Review*, December 1999. Reprinted with permission from *New Oxford Review* and the author.

It is hard to tell the truth about assisted suicide. Or rather, it's hard to get people to listen. Folks generally are about as eager to delve into the issue of assisted suicide as they are to work out the details of their own funeral. It's a delicate and unnerving subject, involving the ultimate issues of life: the reality of human mortality; fears about illness, disability, and old age; and the loss of loved ones to the dark, dank grave. Thus simply getting people to pay close attention to assisted suicide—to grapple with its threat—is often a challenging task.

This is even true of people who are religious or prolife, whose faith informs them that death isn't the end but the beginning. In my work as an anti-euthanasia activist, I have often appeared in front of prolife and religious organizations to speak about assisted suicide. More often than not, event organizers tell me that the audience is one-half to two-thirds the size of their audiences for programs about abortion or some other issue of concern to these communities. This has happened so many times now that it is a clear pattern.

I don't take the empty chairs personally. I understand the emotional dynamic at work. Life is difficult and worrisome enough without visiting the painful realm of assisted suicide. It is difficult, even for deeply religious people, to listen, to heed, and to care enough to become involved. But avoidance of the assisted-suicide issue is a luxury that those who believe in the infinite value of all human life can no longer afford, because battles over assisted suicide are being waged—and more battles planned—throughout the country. Tragically, one major battle has already been lost: Oregon legalized assisted suicide in 1994 and the law went into effect in September 1997. Today in the U.S. a small number of physicians participate actively in their patients' suicide, and it is absolutely legal.

On the bright side, since 1997, when Oregon's voters refused to repeal the state's assisted-suicide law, a broad-based national coalition of diverse groups has formed to oppose the death agenda. Disability-rights activists, advocates for the poor, professional associations in medicine and law, and hospice organizations—all of which tend to be liberal and secular—have joined with Catholics and other religious people and traditional prolife activists to oppose medicalized killing. And this collaboration has borne fruit. Since 1994 five states (Maryland, Rhode Island, Louisiana, Iowa, and Michigan) have passed laws explicitly making assisted suicide a crime, while Virginia outlawed it as a civil wrong, subjecting anyone who assists in a suicide to civil litigation. In November 1998, Michigan's voters rejected an initiative to legalize suicide by an overwhelming 71 to 29 percent. (That's the same state that put the murderer Jack Kevorkian in prison where he belongs.) National public opinion polls that used to show consistent popular support for assisted suicide in the 70 percent range now generally show support in the mid-to-high 50th percentile. Still, the death tide is powerful and must be contained and further reversed. . . .

It Is Legal to Refuse Medical Treatment

Too many people support assisted suicide because they have watched in horror as loved ones were hooked up to medical machines and kept alive against their desires when they were in the last days of life. The threat of such abuse is fading as the economics of medicine moves inexorably toward managed care in which profits are made from cutting costs rather than providing medical services. Still, for many non-ideological supporters of assisted suicide, "being hooked up to machines" is the prime concern.

Frequently, in my experience, supporters of assisted suicide turn into opponents once they learn that they have the legal right to refuse unwanted medical treatment—even if refusing care will probably lead to their deaths. If a dying person doesn't want a ventilator or kidney dialysis, he doesn't have to have it. If he wants to die at home instead of in a hospital, he can. No one need commit suicide because of fears of falling prey to high-tech medicine.

Declining unwanted medical treatment is the philosophical foundation of the hospice movement—which helps dying people die without killing them. In hospice care, machines are out, high-tech medicine is out, surgery other than as an elective procedure to relieve symptoms is out, impersonal medical institutions are out. Nurturing is in. Pain management and symptom control are in, as are spiritual and social services. The goal of a hospice is not to extend life but to help dying people live out their days in comfort and dignity and to care for them in a setting of unconditional love. Hospice care works so well that it is quite common for the dying person to declare that the experience of heading toward death is a "blessing." There, then, is true death with dignity—and nobody gives anybody a lethal dose of poison.

Pain Control Is Not the Same as Assisted Suicide

Assisted-suicide advocates often try to create a false moral equivalence between the medical control of pain and so-called mercy killing. Their argument goes something like this: Since some people's deaths are hastened by the powerful medications often required for effective palliation [pain control], and since such pain control is considered moral and ethical based on the "principle of double-effect," then assisted suicide should also be viewed as moral and ethical because the intention of assisted suicide is similarly to alleviate suffering. There's only one problem with this argument. It completely misapplies the principle of double-effect.

Double-effect recognizes that there are occasions when a person may intend to do a good thing while recognizing that a bad thing *might* occur despite all of his good intentions. Even if the bad outcome then occurs, so long as the original intention was good, then the action is deemed morally acceptable.

In order for the double-effect principle to apply—meaning an act that produces a bad result is still considered to be ethical—four conditions must be met:

1. The action taken (in this case, treating pain and relieving suffering) is "good" or morally neutral.
2. The bad effect (in this case, death) may be a risk but it is not intended.
3. The good effect cannot be brought about by means of the bad effect.
4. There is a proportionately grave reason to perform the act (in this case, the alleviation of severe pain) and to risk therein the bad effect.

If properly applied pain control accidentally hastens a patient's death, the palliative act remains ethical because the bad effect—death—was not intended. On the other hand, assisted suicide *intentionally causes death* as the means of alleviating suffering. Thus, it fails to measure up to the principle of double-effect and therefore remains an immoral and unethical act.

Pain control, like all medical treatments, whether surgery, chemotherapy, or having a simple medical test, can have unintended lethal side effects. Assisted suicide, on the other hand, has but one intention—the death of the patient—that should not be confused with its purported motive—an end to suffering. Assisted suicide is thus a profound violation of the "do no harm" values of Hippocratic medicine.

Assisted Suicide Would Not Be Limited to the Terminally Ill

Legalizing assisted suicide for people who are diagnosed with a terminal illness is wrong. To authorize doctors to dispatch dying people sends the insidious cultural message that the lives of sick and dying people are of little use or value. Kathryn Tucker, an attorney for the assisted-suicide advocacy group Compassion in Dying, once argued in court that the state had little interest in protecting the lives of terminally ill people from suicide because their lives are not "viable." On the other hand, most opponents of assisted suicide understand that if we are to value all human life we must treat all people equally. Whether the desire to self-destruct is caused by serious illness, a broken heart, or mental illness, common decency and compassion call for suicide prevention, not the abandonment to death-facilitation.

That being said, most assisted-suicide advocates do not want to limit death-doctor services to people who are terminally ill. Advocates are well aware that popular support for assisted suicide evaporates when the legalization criteria involve chronically ill, elderly, depressed, or disabled people. This presents an acute political problem for them: They want a broad license for medicalized killing but they know they can't promote it openly because they will lose substantial public support.

As a result, advocates resort to using vague and expandable language. In December 1997, shortly after the Oregon law went into effect, the organization called Compassion in Dying of Washington released a fundraising letter. The group had been a key participant in legalizing assisted suicide in Oregon, and was now ready to move its death agenda to the next level, writing to supporters that they needed increased funding because:

> We have expanded our mission to include not only termi-
> nally ill individuals, but also persons with *incurable illnesses*
> which will eventually lead to a terminal diagnosis. The need
> for increased funding is even more crucial (emphasis added).

"Incurable illnesses which will eventually lead to a terminal diagnosis" covers a far broader array of maladies than
terminal illness, and may include asymptomatic HIV infection, multiple sclerosis, diabetes, emphysema, early-stage
cancer, asthma, and many other diseases.

A DISPOSABLE SOCIETY

Mike Ramirez. Reprinted by permission of Copley News Service.

Similarly, on July 27, 1998, the Hemlock Society, perhaps
the nation's largest assisted-suicide advocacy group, issued a
press release calling for the legalization of assisted suicide
for people with "incurable conditions." The use of the word
"incurable" was intentional. Most people think "terminal"
when they hear "incurable," but the terms are not synonyms.
Arthritis is incurable but not terminal. Often paraplegia is
too. Herpes, too, cannot be cured.

The true agenda of the assisted-suicide movement came into focus in October 1998, when the World Federation of Right to Die Societies—an organization consisting of the world's foremost euthanasia advocacy groups—issued its "Zurich Declaration" after its biannual convention. The Declaration urged that people "suffering severe and enduring *distress* [should be eligible] to receive medical help to die" (emphasis added). Finally, the actual goal of the assisted-suicide movement is revealed: death on demand for anyone with more than a transitory wish to die. . . .

Assisted Suicide Is Not Working Well in Oregon

Assisted suicide in Oregon operates in a shroud of state-imposed secrecy. What little we know comes from the press releases of assisted-suicide advocacy groups and from a study published in the *New England Journal of Medicine* which purported to shed light on the law's actual workings. Assisted-suicide advocates claimed that the *NEJM* report validated their cause. But a close reading reveals that the worries of assisted-suicide opponents are entirely justified.

Fifteen people reportedly committed assisted suicide legally in Oregon in 1998. (The study acknowledges that there is no way to know if this number includes all of the actual assisted suicides. While the law requires doctors to report all assisted suicides, it does not punish doctors who fail to comply.) According to the report, *none* of the dead patients committed assisted suicide because of intractable pain or suffering that could not be otherwise alleviated. Rather, those who committed the act did so based primarily on fears of future dependency. This represents a dramatic expansion of the types of medical conditions that assisted-suicide advocates had told Oregon's citizens the law would end. These disturbing results demonstrate that assisted suicide, rather than being a rare event resorted to only in cases of extreme medical urgency, will expand steadily. . . .

Disability-rights advocates point out that allowing assisted suicide based upon fear of needing help going to the toilet or bathing or doing other daily-life activities will involve far more disabled people than those who are actually dying. They also note that, like other difficulties in life, dependency is a circumstance to which people adjust with time. To accept that worries about the potential need for living assistance are a reason for doctors to write lethal prescriptions is to put disabled people at material risk and to send the message that such lives are not worth living. That is why nine national disability-rights organizations have come out strongly against legalizing assisted suicide, and not one such national group supports it.

The *NEJM* study also reports that the people who committed assisted suicide had "shorter" relationships with the doctors who prescribed lethally than did a group of control patients who died naturally under their physicians' care. The exact time difference is not given but we do know from earlier media reports that a patient's relationship with a death-doctor is likely to be quite short. The first woman to commit assisted suicide in Oregon had a *two-and-a-half-week* relationship with the doctor who wrote her lethal prescription. Her own doctor had refused to assist her suicide, as had a second doctor—who diagnosed her with depression. So she went to an advocacy group and was referred to a death-doctor willing to do the deed. Hers was not a unique case, as the report shows. This isn't careful medical practice, it is rampant Kevorkianism.

Assisted Suicide Would Really Be About Money

In the end, assisted suicide would be less about "choice" than about profits in the health-care system and cutting the costs of health care to government. This is the conclusion of none other than Derek Humphry and pro-euthanasia attorney Mary Clement, who in their book *Freedom to Die* admit that cost-containment may become the bottom-line justification for physician-assisted suicide (PAS):

> A rational argument can be made for allowing PAS in order to offset the amount society and family spend on the ill. . . . Since the largest medical expenses are incurred in the final days and weeks of life, the hastened demise of people with only a short time left would free resources for others. Hundreds of billions of dollars could benefit those patients who not only *can* be cured but who *want* to live.

Imagine a health-care system in which the profit incentives favor killing as the best "treatment" for cancer, Lou Gehrig's disease, multiple sclerosis, spinal injury, Alzheimer's disease, and the many other medical conditions that in some way touch us all. Imagine the money to be made by for-profit HMOs if they are spared the expense of caring for such patients until the end of their natural lives. (The drugs for an assisted suicide cost only about $40, whereas it might cost tens of thousands of dollars to treat the patient properly.) And imagine the potential for abuse and coercion in a health-care system in which killing can lead to greater profits, not to mention increased stock values and performance bonuses. Since our moral values often follow our pocketbooks, the result would be a profound devolution of our culture and of the ethics of medical practice.

To legalize physician-assisted suicide would be to take up again the practices of ancient societies that exposed disabled infants on the hillside and left the elderly and infirm by the side of the road. Protecting the lives of vulnerable people against medicalized killing is essential not only to this country but also to the world. After all, if we can export rock music and consumerism, we can certainly export the twisted values of Jack Kevorkian. That would be a tragic fate for a country that Abraham Lincoln once called the last best hope of earth.

*"If a person fails [to draft an advance
directive] . . . , he forfeits, by default, his
right to avoid the ultimate imprisonment
in a functionless body."*

Advance Directives Protect the Right to Die

Don Udall

Advance directives are documents that record an individual's
wishes about life support in the event that he or she becomes
unable to communicate. In the following viewpoint, Don
Udall encourages people to draft advance directives if they
wish to avoid the prospect of physicians performing unwanted
life-sustaining measures on them. Advance directives can ensure that the dying will not linger in a vegetative state for
years attached to feeding tubes and other life-support technologies. Udall is a surgeon in Newport Beach, California.

As you read, consider the following questions:
1. What percentage of citizens make known their wishes
   about end-of-life care, according to Udall?
2. How long was Morris Udall kept alive by a feeding tube,
   according to the author?
3. According to Udall, about how many patients are
   currently in permanent vegetative states?

Reprinted from Don A. Udall, "Mo Udall's Ordeal Could Inspire More Use of
Living Wills," *Arizona Republic*, January 27, 1999. Reprinted with permission from
the author.

Arizona's Mo Udall died a sad and lengthy death in December 1998. Yet Mo's many years in a hospital bed resulted in greater research regarding Parkinson's disease. In addition, his last years poignantly illustrate the need for the increased use of living wills/advance directives.

As a practicing physician, I have conversed with many in our family and written on this subject for more than 18 months, since I last paid a sad visit to Mo's frail, broken, horribly contracted body. Mo, a former Arizona congressman, died December 12, 1998. He had hardly uttered a word since May 1991, after a fall and head injury, being unaware of his person or even place or time.

A Dreaded Tragedy

One of the most dreaded tragedies in life is to enter a lingering vegetative state and to have this state prolonged by the "miracles" of modern medicine. This is perhaps the ultimate imprisonment, a claustrophobia nightmare, when there is virtually no hope for recovery. If a person fails to have made a Health Care Durable Power of Attorney/ Advance Directive for family agents, he forfeits, by default, his right to avoid the ultimate imprisonment in a functionless body.

Though well-intentioned, doctors and scientists have created a "societal monster." Advances of medicine coupled with the neglect of lawyers and doctors to foster and provide simpler, standardized Healthcare Advance Directives (HADs) have evolved to produce a national tragedy.

Less than one-fifth of our citizens spell out their concerns regarding end-of-life care. Without these patient directives, we doctors are bound by the Hippocratic oath to maintain life, at all costs, regardless of the patient's specific circumstances. In most states, to not do so could be treated by local authorities as a crime.

Adversity and affliction sometimes serve to inspire a paradigm shift in our thinking. Perhaps the tragic neurological illness that afflicted one of our most respected recent national leaders, Morris Udall, will serve as a catalyst to create such a beneficial shift in attitude and encourage more people to establish their health care power of attorney.

Mo Udall served with distinction and unquestioned integrity from 1961 to1991 in the House of Representatives before finally being forced to retire due to Parkinson's disease. Permanently silenced by his Parkinsonism, which attacks the brain's ability to think and reason in only about one-third of cases, he had been fed through a stomach tube while strapped in a hospital bed for more than six years. He existed in a lingering near-vegetative state with minimal, if any, consciousness, a "miracle" of modern medicine.

The Need to Talk in Advance About Death

Talking in advance about death is clearly no salve for the pain of losing a mother, a child or a friend. But when people avoid the subject, many health care experts say, dying often becomes even more traumatic to patients and those caring for them, compounding the loss that even the most careful planning can never erase.

People die after undergoing lengthy and frequently painful treatments that they never told anyone they did not want. Families are forced to make critical decisions for loved ones who are no longer mentally competent and who never voiced their wishes. And doctors—many of whom do not initiate discussions about care at the end of life even with terminally ill patients—treat the dying not knowing whether their patients would consider their care too aggressive or not aggressive enough.

Esther B. Fein, *New York Times*, March 5, 1996.

Yet Mo served us even in his adversity and prolonged ordeal. His tragic story demonstrates the need for every adult to have a simple, inexpensive one-page document called a Healthcare Advance Directive (living will). With such an advance directive to his doctors, Mo could have prevented the anguish and unparalleled loss of dignity that racked his family these past years of artificially extended "life."

Concerned Americans for a Responsible Exit with Dignity

Only 17 percent of Americans have such advance directives. Morris King Udall was one of my childhood heroes and in his honor, I am starting a foundation to promote such advance directives. We will call it CARED, Concerned Americans for a Responsible Exit with Dignity.

This foundation should profoundly benefit our whole society and will prevent untold grief and anguish, as well as billions in needless health care expense. Ultimately, the federal government could be the repository for the registration of these Healthcare Advance Directives in concert with the state's department of motor vehicles, which already register organ donor cards. Eventually we may even see a shortened form on the back of one's drivers' license as a reference to the longer registered form.

There are about 35,000 patients with the diagnosis of permanent vegetative state in which there are only a few brain stem reflexes including breathing and intestinal function. There are possibly an additional five times that number with similar afflictions, such as Mo's, with more complex brain stem functions, who have the diagnosis of minimally conscious state with little, if any, thinking ability. The emotional toll is horrendous, and the financial cost of caring for these patients is staggering—easily $40 billion per year. This cost will grow dramatically with aging of the baby boomers.

As a physician, taxpayer and member of only one of many suffering families, I hope all readers will see the wisdom of creating a Healthcare Advance Directive. Moreover, had he been able, I believe Mo Udall would have encouraged every American to support a national endeavor to foster the promulgation and widespread implementation of this important legal document.

"The right to die with dignity looks very much like the right to commit murder."

Living Wills Do Not Protect the Right to Live

Murray N. Rothbard

Living wills—or advance directives, as others call them—do not protect the rights of those who wish to receive life-sustaining treatments, argues Murray N. Rothbard in the following viewpoint. Although living wills supposedly enable individuals to document their decision to accept or decline life support should they become comatose, these decisions are not always honored. Medical authorities seeking to cut costs may prematurely end the life of a person who wished to be kept alive, Rothbard contends. Rothbard, who died in 1995, was a libertarian philosopher and economist.

As you read, consider the following questions:
1. How does Helga Wanglie's case illustrate the trouble with living wills, in Rothbard's opinion?
2. What entity was paying Helga Wanglie's medical costs, according to the author?
3. According to Rothbard, how has Derek Humphry contradicted himself on his statements about a patient's right to live or die?

Reprinted from Murray N. Rothbard, "The Right to Kill, with Dignity?" *Rothbard-Rockwell Report*, March 1999. Reprinted with permission from the Center for Libertarian Studies.

For a long time now we have been subjected to a barrage of pro-death propaganda by Left-Liberals, and by their cheering squad, Left, or Modal, Libertarians. The "right to die," the "right to die with dignity" (whatever that means), the right to get someone to assist you in suicide, the "right to euthanasia," etc. Up till now, Left-Liberals have at least appeared to be scrupulous in stressing the crucial importance of consent by the killed victim, because *otherwise* the right to die with dignity looks very much like the right to commit murder. For what is compulsory euthanasia but murder, pure and simple?

But now the mask has begun to slip. One of the great enthusiasms of the right-to-die forces has long been the Living Will, in which the prospective candidate for euthanasia signs a form requesting his family, medical authorities, etc., to pull the plug under specified conditions. I have long been queasy about the consensual bona fides of the right-to-diers and have wondered what would happen if somebody wrote a Living Will that was spunky instead of spineless, that insistently favored his own life as against his death.

The Overriding of Living Wills

Now we know, and the answer, to say the least, is not good. Helga Wanglie, an elderly lady in Minneapolis, wrote a Living Will, but she opted for being kept alive if she lapsed into a vegetative state. Now 87, she is indeed in such a state, and her husband, respecting Helga's wishes in realizing that only while there is life can there be hope, is anxious to respect Helga's wishes and keep her alive. Note, too, that Helga's medical cost is being covered privately, by private health insurance; Helga is no burden on the taxpayer.

So what's the problem? The problem is that the medical authorities, in their wisdom, have decided that since Helga's case is hopeless, they should have the right to pull the plug, overriding the wishes of Helga on this issue. But what are the medical authorities, whose very profession pledges them to keep patients alive to the best of their ability, advocating here if it is not mere murder? The Minnesota doctors, having decided that Helga Wanglie is not fit to live, propose to murder her, and they, and other liberals, are sneering at the

Wanglies for being backward Neanderthals in trying to affirm her life. Will somebody explain to me how this attitude differs from that of Nazi doctors, with their zeal to exterminate people whose lives they considered unfit?

The right to kill seems to be the established medical position. Thus, Minnesota "medical ethicist" Dr. Steven Miles: "We are certain this person cannot change from her present condition. Shouldn't we be making sure that we're responsible in allocating the resources . . . to keep costs down for everybody?" Notice the paramount consideration given to the collective "we," with individuals not allowed to decide their own costs, and with the Doctor, long professionally accustomed to playing God, now playing Satan.

Lifesaving Treatment Is Frequently Denied

Most of the cases that have reached the courts have concluded that the patient's best interests are served by cutting off life support. In fact, according to a survey of doctors published in the July/August 1991 *Journal of General Internal Medicine*, one in three doctors believed that "regardless of the patient's treatment preferences," doctors should be able to decide whether or not to give cardiopulmonary resuscitation for patients "who suffer from severe chronic illness or terminal disease."

A nursing home study in the March 1991 *New England Journal of Medicine* found in over two-thirds of the cases in which advance directives were not followed by the nursing home and medical staff, the patients were denied treatment they had requested. Nearly 1 in 5 patients with advance directives were denied life-saving treatment they said they wanted. By contrast, in only 7 percent of cases was treatment provided against the wishes of the patients as expressed in their advance directives.

Burke Balch, *World and I*, February 1996.

Maryland University professor Oliver Childs declaims, "Despite the feelings of the family . . . the final decision should be made by the medical authorities. Prolonging life creates a burden on family and friends. . . . It can also be very expensive." Expenses which the burdened family is not to be allowed to shoulder.

No social-medical problem is complete without a pronouncement from neo-conservative medical economist Harry Schwartz, for three decades an editorial writer for the *New York Times*. Schwartz sneers at the "values of individual autonomy and the sanctity of human life" which have to give way to more important values, such as that health resources are limited, and that health care must be allocated rationally. Schwartz is nothing if not hard-nosed: "the harsh truth is that most of these people will never wake up. So, the basic problem is why we let so many vegetables receive useless care for so long." The problem, opines Schwartz, is that our health insurance systems, private as well as public, are "too mindlessly generous." Schwartz concludes, "The time to end this idiocy is now."

Contradictory Positions

Our final specimen is Derek Humphry, head of the Hemlock Society, the most venerable of right to suicide groups, and careful up to now to stress consent. Where does he stand on the case of Helga Wanglie? Humphry begins by saying that patients "should always have the right of choice to live or die," and if they are in a persistent vegetative state, their families should decide. OK, so what about Helga Wanglie? Here is Humphry's new and contradictory position: "if overwhelming medical opinion says treatment is pointless, courts should arbitrate disputes between doctors and families." Now just a minute: where do courts get the right to decide life or death? Does government have more of a right to commit murder than doctors, or what? And on what principles are the courts supposed to decide that "arbitration"?

No, the mask is off, and Doctor Assisted Death and Mr. Liberal Death With Dignity, and all the rest of the crew turn out to be simply Doctor and Mister Murder. Watch out Mr. and Ms. America: liberal humanists, lay and medical, are not only out to regulate your lives, and to fleece your pocketbooks. They're out to kill you! Libertarians, as embodied in the sainted "Nolan Chart," have always assumed that conservatives are in favor of economic liberty, whereas liberals are in favor of civil, or personal liberty. *This* is "personal liberty"?

The excuses of these killers is that far more important

than prolonging life is the "quality of life." But what if a key part of preserving and enhancing that quality is getting rid of this crew of murdering liberals, people whom Isabel Paterson, with wonderful perception and prophetic insight, termed "the humanitarian with the guillotine"? What then? So where do we sign up to assist *their* death?

| "We must recognize that suicides and requests for assisted suicide may be motivated by love. Sometimes, it's simply the only loving thing to do."

The Terminally Ill May Have a Duty to Die

John Hardwig

John Hardwig teaches medical ethics and social and political philosophy at East Tennessee State University in Johnson City. In the following viewpoint, Hardwig argues that the terminally ill sometimes have a duty to die. This duty is prompted when continuing medical treatments would place devastating emotional and financial burdens on a dying person's family and loved ones. A dutiful decision to die, though tragic, can be a responsible and loving choice, Hardwig maintains.

As you read, consider the following questions:
1. According to Hardwig, why are people often appalled at the notion that the ill may have a duty to die?
2. How does the "individualistic fantasy about ourselves" influence discussions about assisted suicide, in the author's opinion?
3. According to a recent study cited by Hardwig, about what percentage of families loses all their savings after caring for a dying family member?

Excerpted from John Hardwig, "Dying at the Right Time: Reflections on Assisted and Unassisted Suicide," from www.etsu-tn.edu/philos/faculty/john/dying.htm, September 1996. Reprinted with permission from the author.

L et us begin with two observations about chronic illness and death:

1. Death does not always come at the right time. We are all aware of the tragedies involved when death comes too soon. We are afraid that it might come too soon for us. By contrast, we may sometimes be tempted to deny that death can come too late—wouldn't everyone want to live longer? But in our more sober moments, most of us know perfectly well that death can come too late.

2. Discussions of death and dying usually proceed as if death came only to hermits—or others who are all alone. But most of the time, death is a death in the family. We are connected to family and loved ones. We are sustained by these connections. They are a major part of what makes life worth living for most of us.

Because of these connections, when death comes too soon, the tragedy is often two-fold: a tragedy both for the person who is now dead and for those of us to whom she was connected. We grieve both for our loved one who is gone and for ourselves who have lost her. On one hand, there is the unrealized good that life would have been for the dead person herself—what she could have become, what she could have experienced, what she wanted for herself. On the other, there is the contribution she would have made to others and the ways *their* lives would have been enriched by her.

Death Can Come Too Late

We are less familiar with the idea that death can come too late. But here, too, the tragedy can be two-fold. Death can come too late because of what living on means to the person herself. There are times when someone does not (or would not) want to live like this, times when she believes she would be better off dead. At times like these, suicide or assisted suicide becomes a perfectly rational choice, perhaps even the best available option for her. We are then forced to ask, Does someone have a right to die? Assisted suicide may then be an act of compassion, no more than relieving her misery.

There are also, sadly, times when death comes too late because *others*—family and loved ones—would be better off if someone were dead. (Better off overall, despite the loss of a loved one.) Since lives are deeply intertwined, the lives of the rest of the family can be dragged down, impoverished, compromised, perhaps even ruined because of what they must go through if she lives on. When death comes too late because of the effect of someone's life on her loved ones, we are, I think, forced to ask, Can someone have a duty to die? Suicide may then be an attempt to do what is right; it may be the only loving thing to do. Assisted suicide would then be helping someone do the right thing.

Most professional ethicists—philosophers, theologians, and bioethicists—react with horror at the very idea of a duty to die. Many of them even argue that euthanasia and physician-assisted suicide should not be legalized because then some people might somehow get the idea that they have a duty to die. To this way of thinking, someone who got that idea could only be the victim of vicious social pressure or perverse moral reasoning. But when I ask my classes for examples of times when death would come too late, one of the first conditions students always mention is: "when I become a burden to my family." I think there is more moral wisdom here than in the dismay of these ethicists. . . .

The Duty to Die

I may well one day have a duty to die, a duty most likely to arise out of my connections with my family and loved ones. Sometimes preserving my life can only devastate the lives of those who care about me. I do not believe I am idiosyncratic, morbid or morally perverse in believing this. I am trying to take steps to prepare myself mentally and spiritually to make sure that I will be able to take my life if I should one day have such a duty. I need to prepare myself; it might be a very difficult thing for me to do.

Our individualistic fantasy about ourselves sometimes leads us to imagine that lives are separate and unconnected, or that they could be so if we chose. If lives were unconnected, then things that happen in my life would not or need not affect others. And if others were not (much) affected by my life, I would have no duty to consider the impact of my life on others. I would then be morally free to choose whatever life and death I prefer for myself. I certainly would have no duty to die when I would prefer to live.

Most discussions of assisted suicide and euthanasia implicitly share this individualistic fantasy: they just ignore the fact that people are connected and lives intertwined. As a result, they approach issues of life or death as if the only person affected is the one who lives or dies. They mistakenly assume the pivotal issue is simply whether the person *herself* prefers not to live like this and whether *she herself* would be better off dead.

But this is morally obtuse. The fact is we are not a race of hermits—most of us are connected to family and loved ones. We prefer it that way. We would not want to be all alone, especially when we are seriously ill, as we age, and when we are dying. But being with others is not all benefits and pleasures; it brings responsibilities, as well. For then what happens to us and the choices we make can dramatically affect the lives of our loved ones. It is these connections that can, tragically, generate obligations to die, as continuing to live takes too much of a toll on the lives of those connected to us.

The lives of our loved ones can, we know, be seriously compromised by caring for us. The burdens of providing care or even just supervision 24 hours/day, 7 days/week are often overwhelming. But it can also be emotionally devastating simply to be married to a spouse who is increasingly distant, uncommunicative, unresponsive, foreign and unreachable. A local newspaper tells the story of a woman with Alzheimer's who came running into her den screaming: "That man's trying to have sex with me! He's trying to have sex with me! Who *is* that man?!" That man was her loving husband of more than 40 years who had devoted the past 10 years of his life to caring for her. How terrible that experience must have been for her. But how terrible those years must be for him, too.

Financial Burdens

We must also acknowledge that the lives of our loved ones can also be devastated just by having to *pay* for health care for us. A recent study documented the financial aspects of caring for a dying member of a family. Only those who had illnesses severe enough to give them less than a 50% chance to live six more months were included in this study. When these patients survived their initial hospitalization and were discharged, about ⅓ required considerable caregiving from their families, in 20% of cases a family member had to quit work or make some other major lifestyle change, almost ⅓ of these families lost all of their savings, and just under 30% lost a major source of income.

A Public Policy Tragedy

We do not have a "right to die." Human beings are mortal. Death is neither a right nor an option. Yet, there is a public policy tragedy in our misconception. Money desperately needed elsewhere in society is being spent on marginal and low benefit medicine throughout the system, but particularly on the dying process. No other society would take a 90-year-old with congestive heart disease or terminal cancer out of a nursing home and put him into an intensive care unit. My wife and I were recently at the bedside of a 93-year-old man with three fatal diseases (metastic cancer of the prostate, end-stage kidney failure, and he had just been brought into the intensive care unit with a serious stroke). Massive resources were being poured into this gentleman, while blocks away people were going without primary care and kids were going without vaccinations.

Richard D. Lamm, *Cambridge Quarterly of Healthcare Ethics*, 1997.

A chronic illness or debilitating injury in a family is a misfortune. It is, most often, nobody's fault; no one is responsible for this illness or injury. But then we face choices about how we will respond to this misfortune. That's where the responsibility comes in and fault can arise. Those of us with families and loved ones always have a responsibility not to make selfish or self-centered decisions about our lives. We should not do just what we want or just what is best for us. Often, we should choose in light of what is best for all concerned.

Our families and loved ones have obligations to stand by us and to support us through debilitating illness and death. They must be prepared to make sacrifices to respond to an illness in the family. We are well aware of this responsibility and most families meet it rather well. In fact, families deliver more than 80% of the long-term care in this country, almost always at great personal cost.

But responsibility in a family is not a one-way street. When we become seriously ill or debilitated, we too may have to make sacrifices. There are limits to what we can ask our loved ones to do to support us, even in sickness. There are limits to what they should be prepared to do for us—only rarely and for a limited period of time should they do all they can for us.

Somehow we forget that sick, infirm, and dying adults also have obligations to their families and loved ones: a responsibility, for example, to try to protect the lives of loved ones from serious threats or greatly impoverished quality, or an obligation to avoid making choices that will jeopardize or seriously compromise their futures. Our obligations to our loved ones must be taken into consideration in making decisions about the end of life. It is out of these responsibilities that a duty to die can develop.

Tragically, sometimes the best thing you can do for your loved ones is to remove yourself from their lives. And the only way you can do that may be to remove yourself from existence. This is not a happy thought. Yet we must recognize that suicides and requests for assisted suicide may be motivated by love. Sometimes, it's simply the only loving thing to do.

> *"The doctor must place the interests of patients first, above monetary considerations, his or her own self-interest and the interests of society."*

The Terminally Ill Should Not Be Pressured to Die

Part I: Nat Hentoff; Part II: Miguel A. Faria Jr.

The authors of the following two-part viewpoint question the principles of bioethicists who argue that the severely ill should die to relieve society of costly health-care burdens. In Part I, syndicated columnist Nat Hentoff points out that such arguments could wrongly pressure sick and elderly people into believing that they have a duty to die. In Part II, Miguel A. Faria Jr. argues that the concept of a patient's duty to die undermines the Hippocratic oath and promotes a misguided form of health-care rationing. Faria is editor-in-chief of *Medical Sentinel*, a publication of the Association of American Physicians and Surgeons in Macon, Georgia.

As you read, consider the following questions:

1. According to Hentoff, what challenge did former Colorado governor Richard Lamm issue to American citizens?
2. What does the Hippocratic oath clearly state, according to Faria?
3. In Faria's opinion, why are physicians often unable to effectively treat pain in terminally ill patients?

Part I: Reprinted from Nat Hentoff, "The Right to Die? Now It's Your Duty," *Los Angeles Times*, June 2, 1997. Reprinted with permission from the author. Part II: Reprinted from Miguel A. Faria Jr., "Advocate for Pain Relief, Not 'Duty to Die,'" *Medical Tribune*, November 18, 1999. Reprinted with permission from *Medical Tribune* and the author.

I

While he was governor of Colorado, Richard Lamm became, for a time, a troubling national presence. Not as a result of his politics but because of the challenge he issued to the citizenry in every state. At an autumnal age, he said, it is a moral responsibility to make room for the young. As leaves fall from the trees in the fall, so old people have a duty to die.

The governor and I were asked to debate this proposition at Pennsylvania State University. When we arrived at the hotel in the afternoon, he urgently asked the desk clerk if there was a gym nearby where he could have his customary workout. It occurred to me that he wanted to delay the day, as best he could, when his own leaves would fall.

Dying as a Utilitarian Imperative

As a consequence of the current national debate on physician-assisted suicide, its opponents have predicted that if assisted suicide is legalized, people whose illnesses are costly and long-term may be convinced they have a duty to die. Feeling guilty because of the burden they have become to their families, they—with suicide now approved by society—may ask their doctors to help them die.

Now, in certain bioethical circles, the morality of dying as a utilitarian imperative is being advanced. Those who mocked Lamm's advice to go responsibly into the good night may have been premature.

The *Hastings Center Report* is one of the more respected journals dealing with the nature of human nature and medical ethics. The leading article on the cover of its March/April 1997 issue is John Hardwig's "Is There a Duty to Die?" The author teaches medical ethics and social political philosophy at East Tennessee State University.

At the start, Hardwig declares that "modern medicine and an individualistic culture have seduced many [into believing] that they have a right to health care and a right to live, despite the burdens and costs to our families and society."

Hardwig recognizes that there already is a legal right to refuse life-prolonging medical treatment. But, he claims, "a duty to die can go well beyond that. . . . There may be a fairly common responsibility to end one's life in the absence of any terminal illness." Indeed, "there can be a duty to die even when one would prefer to live."

After all, "the lives of our loved ones can be seriously compromised by caring for us. . . . There is a sense in which we fail to respect ourselves if, in the face of illness or death, we stoop to choosing just what is best for ourselves."

The Effect on Vulnerable Patients

Years ago, Michigan University law professor Yale Kamisar predicted that with the coming of assisted suicide, precisely this kind of argument could well persuade vulnerable patients to let themselves slip into eternity rather than remain a burden.

Hardwig also makes the stern point that as we grow older, the duty to die becomes more compelling because "we will be giving up less . . . we will sacrifice fewer remaining years of life." (Perhaps copies of Walter Huston singing "September Song" may ease the way.)

Hardwig presses on: "To have reached the age of, say, 75 or 80 years without being ready to die is itself a moral failing, the sign of a life out of touch with life's basic realities."

Will octogenarians who are not ready to die be publicly shamed as the moral community shuns them?

There is another criterion for being ready to join the falling leaves in autumn. "A duty to die," says Hardwig, "is more likely when you have already lived a rich and full life. You have already had a full share of the good things life offers." I assume that the chronically poor as well as long-term prisoners are given compensatory time to stay alive.

But there is a way out for most of the rest of us. If, Hardwig says, society is willing to "pay for facilities that provide excellent long-term care (not just health care) for all chronically ill, debilitated, mentally ill or demented people in this country . . . the duty to die would then be virtually eliminated."

Hardwig, however, is a realist: "We Americans seem to be unwilling to pay for this kind of long-term care, except for ourselves and our own." There will be no escaping, then, a duty to die, provided, says Hardwig, we have the courage to die in order to protect our loved ones from the costs, financially and emotionally, of our staying on.

John Hardwig is not alone. I have heard doctors say that certain patients, taking up expensive space in a hospital, have a duty to die because they will never be able to walk out of the hospital. Dr. Jack Kevorkian is his own kind of ethicist, but if his bedside manner were not so startling, he would be seen as not far from the current ready-to-die mainstream.

John Hardwig says, "We fear death too much." My sense is we do not fear bioethicists enough.

II

Since November 1997, when Oregon voters "resoundingly rejected" a repeal of the state's assisted-suicide initiative (which had been narrowly passed in 1994), more and more articles have appeared in the medical literature, including *Medical Tribune*, supporting this concept.

On the eve of possible repeal of the Oregon law, noted ethicist Timothy E. Quill, M.D., professor of medicine at the University of Rochester in New York, stated: "There is a central mission in medicine, I believe, to help people seek a good and meaningful death, at least a tolerable death, and clearly we have a responsibility to be very responsive, critically responsive, if death gets very hard toward the end of this long process." Afterwards, Glenn M. Gordon, M.D., past president of the Oregon Medical Association, said: "Assisted suicide is an issue whose time has come."

Perhaps we should take a second look at the slippery slope of this practice.

Do No Harm?

The Oath of Hippocrates clearly states: "I will prescribe regimen for the good of my patients according to my ability and my judgment and never do harm to anyone. To please no one will I prescribe a deadly drug, nor give advice which may cause his death."

Ostensibly, the main reason for physician-assisted suicide is intractable pain in terminally ill patients. Yet, in the vast majority of patients, pain can be managed if physicians were not fearful of the veritable "police state of medicine" in which physicians are forced to practice medicine. The *Medical Sentinel* published a special report in its July/August 1998 issue dealing with physician prosecutions, particularly in the area of pain management, for "over-prescription" of controlled substances.

Were physicians allowed to practice medicine according to the Oath and tradition of Hippocrates, the fact is there would be no need for physician-assisted suicide and (active) euthanasia. This is the political arena where organized medicine should be fighting.

Mike Smith. Reprinted by permission of United Features Syndicate.

The ethics of Hippocrates implicitly state the doctor must place the interests of patients first, above monetary considerations, his or her own self-interest and the interests of society. To do otherwise is the first step down the slippery slope of euthanasia and rationing by death.

Presently, many physicians serving on ethics committees in various specialties are unwittingly being used to legitimize medical care rationing under the concepts of "death with dignity," "self-determination" and, as East Tennessee State University ethicist John Hardwig, Ph.D., has so frankly stated, a "duty to die" for the misguided proper and rational allocation of finite health-care resources, veiled under the guise of "personal autonomy."

Many physicians have even questioned whether the (individual) patient-based ethics of Hippocrates are still relevant or should be supplanted by utilitarian population-based medicine.

Leo Alexander, M.D., the eminent psychiatrist and chief U.S. medical consultant at the Nuremberg War Crimes trials, has an answer for this dilemma: "If only those whose treatment is worthwhile in terms of prognosis are to be treated, what about the other ones? The doubtful patients are the ones whose recovery appears unlikely, but frequently if treated energetically, they surprise the best prognosticators."

Once the rational allocation of scarce and finite resources enters the decision-making process in the doctor's role as physician, the next logical stop is: Is it worthwhile to do this or that for this type of patient? Dr. Alexander concludes that "from small beginnings" the values of an entire society may be subverted. "Corrosion begins in microscopic proportions."

Periodical Bibliography

The following articles have been selected to supplement the diverse views presented in this chapter. Addresses are provided for periodicals not indexed in the *Readers' Guide to Periodical Literature*, the *Alternative Press Index*, the *Social Sciences Index*, or the *Index to Legal Periodicals and Books*.

Kathryn Casey	"'Let My Husband Die,'" *Ladies' Home Journal*, July 1999.
Dudley Clendinen	"When Death Is a Blessing and Life Is Not," *New York Times*, February 5, 1996.
Ezekiel J. Emanuel	"Death's Door," *New Republic*, May 17, 1999.
Christine J. Gardner	"Severe Mercy in Oregon," *Christianity Today*, June 14, 1999.
Erica Goode	"Terminal Cancer Patients' Will to Live Is Found to Fluctuate," *New York Times*, September 4, 1999.
Herbert Hendin	"Physician-Assisted Suicide: What Next?" *Responsive Community*, Fall 1997. Available from 2020 Pennsylvania Ave. NW, Suite 282, Washington, DC 20077-2910.
Kevin Irvine	"Over My Dead Body," *POZ*, January 1998. Available from 349 West 12th St., New York, NY 10014-1721.
Norman G. Levinsky	"Advance Directives vs. Patient Choice," *Consumers' Research Magazine*, October 1996.
David B. McCurdy	"Saying What We Mean," *Christian Century*, July 17–24, 1996.
Paul R. McHugh	"Dying Made Easy," *Commentary*, February 1999.
Kathleen Dean Moore	"Do I Kill My Father?" *Commonweal*, June 19, 1998.
Betty Rollin	"Last Rights," *Ms.*, August/September 1999.
John Shelby Spong	"In Defense of Assisted Suicide," *Human Quest*, May/June 1996. Available from 4300 NW 23rd Ave., Box 203, Gainesville, FL 32614-7050.
Adam Wolfson	"Killing Off the Dying?" *Public Interest*, Spring 1998.

For Further Discussion

Chapter 1

1. Marilyn Webb extols the benefits of hospice, arguing that hospice care attends to the largely ignored psychological and spiritual needs of terminally ill patients. Felicia Ackerman, on the other hand, criticizes the hospice movement for promoting principles that may be unacceptable to some terminally ill people. In your opinion, do the potential benefits of hospice outweigh its possible drawbacks? Why or why not? Use evidence from the text to support your answer.

2. Faye Girsh advocates the legalization of physician-assisted suicide. In her viewpoint, she discusses the case of a terminal cancer patient who contacted the Hemlock Society to help her find a physician to supply her with a lethal dose, even though assisted suicide was illegal in her state. In your opinion, was it ethical for the Hemlock Society to provide such information to this patient? Why or why not?

3. In your opinion, which viewpoint in this chapter offered the most helpful suggestions for improving the care of the terminally ill? Which viewpoint offered the least helpful suggestions? Cite the text in explaining your answer.

Chapter 2

1. The American Pain Society maintains that the treatment of the painful symptoms of terminal illness should take precedence over the promotion of physician-assisted suicide. Bobbie Farsides agrees that the terminally ill should have a right to effective pain management, but contends that physician-assisted suicide should be an option for those whose symptoms do not respond to medical treatment. Which author do you agree with, and why?

2. Kirsten Backstrom argues that the pain associated with serious illness should not necessarily be avoided because it may "allow us to see beyond ourselves to something larger and deeper." Backstrom suffered from Hodgkin's lymphoma, and though her life was threatened, she did not die of the illness. In your opinion, is Backstrom qualified to draw conclusions about the suffering associated with terminal illness? Why or why not?

3. Jerome P. Kassirer and Robert L. Maginnis disagree about the need to legalize medical marijuana for the chronically or terminally ill. Kassirer is the editor of the *New England Journal of*

Medicine; Maginnis is an analyst for the Family Research Council, a conservative educational and advocacy organization. Does your awareness of these authors' backgrounds influence your assessment of their arguments? Why or why not? Explain.

Chapter 3

1. Choice in Dying asserts that withdrawing nutritional life support from terminally ill patients often makes the dying process more comfortable. Charles E. Rice maintains that removing feeding tubes can cause gruesomely painful deaths and lead people to prefer euthanasia over the withdrawal of life support. Which author's argument do you find more persuasive? Explain.

2. The authors in this chapter discuss several possible medical responses to the dying process of the terminally ill. Consider each possibility and then list arguments for and against each one. Note whether the arguments are based on facts, values, emotions, or other considerations. If you believe a particular medical response should not be considered at all, explain why.

Chapter 4

1. Erdman B. Palmore contends that terminally ill patients should have the right to assisted suicide. Wesley J. Smith maintains that legalizing assisted suicide minimizes the value of sick and disabled people's lives. Does Smith's viewpoint effectively refute Palmore's arguments? Why or why not?

2. Don Udall and Murray N. Rothbard each employ an anecdotal example to help support their respective arguments for and against living wills, or advance directives. In your opinion, which of these authors uses his anecdote to better effect? Explain.

3. John Hardwig argues that the terminally ill may have a duty to die to protect their loved ones from severe emotional and financial burdens. Do you agree that people with devastating illnesses should hasten their deaths to offset familial hardships? Why or why not? Use evidence from the text to support your answer.

Organizations to Contact

The editors have compiled the following list of organizations concerned with the issues debated in this book. The descriptions are derived from materials provided by the organizations. All have publications or information available for interested readers. The list was compiled on the date of publication of the present volume; the information provided here may change. Be aware that many organizations take several weeks or longer to respond to inquiries, so allow as much time as possible.

American Foundation for Suicide Prevention (AFSP)
120 Wall Street, 22nd Floor, New York, NY 10005
(888) 333-2377 • fax: (212) 363-6237
e-mail: rfabrika@afsp.org • website: www.afsp.org
Formerly known as the American Suicide Foundation, the AFSP supports scientific research on depression and suicide, educates the public and professionals on the recognition and treatment of depressed and suicidal individuals, and provides support programs for those coping with the loss of a loved one to suicide. It opposes the legalization of physician-assisted suicide. AFSP publishes a policy statement on physician-assisted suicide, the newsletter *Crisis*, and the quarterly *Lifesavers*.

American Life League
PO Box 1350, Stafford, VA 22555
(540) 659-4171
e-mail: sysop@all.org • website: www.all.org
The league believes that human life is sacred. It works to educate Americans on the dangers of all forms of euthanasia and opposes legislative efforts that would legalize or increase its incidence. It publishes the bimonthly pro-life magazine *Celebrate Life*; videos; brochures, including "Euthanasia and You" and "Jack Kevorkian: Agent of Death"; and newsletters monitoring abortion- and euthanasia-related legal developments.

American Society of Law, Medicine, and Ethics (ASLME)
765 Commonwealth Ave., Suite 1634, Boston, MA 02215
(617) 262-4990 • fax: (617) 437-7596
e-mail: aslme@bu.edu • website: www.aslme.org
ASLME works to provide scholarship, debate, and critical thought to professionals concerned with legal, health care, policy, and ethical issues. It publishes the *Journal of Law, Medicine, and Ethics* as well as a quarterly newsletter.

Choice in Dying
475 Riverside Dr., New York, NY 10115
(800) 989-WILL • (212) 870-2003 • fax: (212) 870-2040
e-mail: choice@echonyc.com • website: www.choices.org

Choice in Dying is dedicated to fostering communication about end-of-life decisions among the terminally ill, their loved ones, and health care professionals by providing public and professional education about the legal, ethical, and psychological conse-quences of assisted suicide and euthanasia. It publishes the quar-terly newsletter *Choices* and the Question and Answer series, which includes the titles *You and Your Choices*, *Advance Directives*, *Advance Directives and End-of-Life Decisions*, and *Dying at Home*.

Compassion in Dying (CID)
6312 SW Capital Hwy., Suite 415, Portland, OR 97201
(503) 221-9556 • fax: (503) 228-9160
e-mail: info@compassionindying.org
website: www.compassionindying.org

CID believes that dying patients should receive information about all options at the end of life, including those that may has-ten death. It provides information on intensive pain management, comfort or hospice care, and humane, effective aid in dying. CID advocates laws that would make assistance in dying legally avail-able for terminally ill, mentally competent adults, and it publishes a newsletter detailing these efforts.

Death with Dignity
1818 N St. NW, Suite 450, Washington, DC 20036
(202) 530-2900
e-mail: info@deathwithdignity.org
website: www.deathwithdignity.org

Death with Dignity promotes a comprehensive, humane, respon-sive system of care for terminally ill patients. Its members believe that a dying patient's choices should be given the utmost respect and consideration. The center serves as an information resource for the public and the media and promotes strategies for advanc-ing a responsive system of care for terminally ill patients on edu-cational, legal, legislative, and public-policy fronts. It publishes several fact sheets, including *Misconceptions in the Debate on Death with Dignity*, *The Situation in Florida*, *Dying in the U.S.A.: A Call for Public Debate*, and *The Issue: From the Individual's Perspective*, all of which are available in an information package by request.

Dying with Dignity
55 Eglinton Ave. East, Suite 705, Toronto, ON M4P 1G8 Canada
(800) 495-6156 • (416) 486-3998 • fax: (416) 489-9010
e-mail: dwdca@web.net • website: www.web.net/dwd

Dying with Dignity works to improve the quality of dying for all
Canadians in accordance with their own wishes, values, and beliefs. It educates Canadians about their right to choose health care
options at the end of life, provides counseling and advocacy services to those who request them, and builds public support for
voluntary physician-assisted dying. Dying with Dignity publishes
a newsletter and maintains an extensive library of euthanasia-related materials that students may borrow.

Euthanasia Research and Guidance Organization (ERGO)
24829 Norris Ln., Junction City, OR 97448-9559
(541) 998-1873
websites: www.finalexit.org • www.rights.org/~deatnet/ergo.html

ERGO provides information and research findings on physician-
assisted dying to persons who are terminally or hopelessly ill and
wish to end their suffering. Its members counsel dying patients
and develop ethical, psychological, and legal guidelines to help
them and their physicians make life-ending decisions. The organization's publications include *Deciding to Die: What You Should
Consider* and *Assisting a Patient to Die: A Guide for Physicians*.

The Hemlock Society
PO Box 101810, Denver, CO 80250
(800) 247-7421 • (303) 639-1202 • fax: (303) 639-1224
e-mail: hemlock@privatei.com • website: www.hemlock.org

The society believes that terminally ill individuals have the right
to commit suicide. The society publishes books on suicide, death,
and dying, including *Final Exit*, a guide for those suffering with
terminal illnesses and considering suicide. The Hemlock Society
also publishes the newsletter *TimeLines*.

Human Life International (HLI)
4 Family Life Ln., Front Royal, VA 22630
(540) 635-7884 • fax: (540) 635-7363
e-mail: hli@hli.org • website: www.hli.org

HLI categorically rejects abortion and euthanasia and believes assisted suicide is morally unacceptable. It defends the rights of the
unborn, the disabled, and those threatened by euthanasia, and it
provides education, advocacy, and support services. HLI publishes
the monthly newsletters *HLI Reports*, *HLI Update*, and *Deacons Circle*.

International Anti-Euthanasia Task Force (IAETF)
PO Box 760, Steubenville, OH 43952
(740) 282-3810
e-mail: info@iaetf.org • website: www.iaetf.org
The task force opposes euthanasia, assisted suicide, and policies that threaten the lives of the medically vulnerable. IAETF publishes fact sheets and position papers on euthanasia-related topics in addition to the bimonthly newsletter, *IAETF Update*. It analyzes the policies and legislation concerning medical and social work organizations and files *amicus curiae* briefs in major right-to-die cases.

International Association for Near-Death Studies (IANDS)
PO Box 502, East Windsor Hill, CT 06028
(860) 528-5144 • fax: (860) 528-9169
website: www.iands.org/iands
IANDS is a worldwide organization of scientists, scholars, and others who are interested in or who have had near-death experiences. It supports the scientific study of near-death experiences and their implications, fosters communication among researchers on this topic, and sponsors support groups in which people can discuss their near-death experiences. The association publishes the quarterly newsletter *Vital Signs*.

National Hospice Organization (NHO)
1700 Diagonal Rd., Suite 300, Alexandria, VA 22314
(800) 658-8898 • (703) 243-5900 • fax: (703) 525-5762
e-mail: drsnho@cais.org • website: www.nho.org
The organization works to educate the public about the benefits of hospice care for the terminally ill and their families. It seeks to promote the idea that with the proper care and pain medication, the terminally ill can live out their lives comfortably and in the company of their families. The organization opposes euthanasia and assisted suicide. It conducts educational and training programs for administrators and caregivers in numerous aspects of hospice care. It publishes the quarterlies *Hospice Journal* and *Hospice Magazine*, as well as books and monographs.

National Right to Life Committee (NRLC)
419 Seventh St. NW, Suite 500, Washington, DC 20004
(202) 626-8800
e-mail: nrlc@nrlc.org • website: www.nrlc.org
The committee is an activist group that opposes euthanasia and assisted suicide. NRLC publishes the monthly *NRL News* and the four-part position paper "Why We Shouldn't Legalize Assisting Suicide."

Bibliography of Books

Michael Appleton et al. *At Home with Terminal Illness: A Family Guidebook to Hospice in the Home.* Upper Saddle River, NJ: Prentice Hall, 1994.

Lofty L. Basta with Carole Post *A Graceful Exit: Life and Death on Your Own Terms.* New York: Plenum, 1996.

Margaret P. Battin and Arthur G. Lipman, eds. *Drug Use in Assisted Suicide and Euthanasia.* Binghamton, NY: Pharmaceutical Products, 1996.

Phillip L. Berman *The Journey Home: What Near-Death Experiences and Mysticism Teach Us About the Gift of Life.* New York: Pocket, 1998.

Kenneth J. Doka *Living with Life-Threatening Illness: A Guide for Patients, Their Families, and Caregivers.* San Francisco: Jossey-Bass, 1998.

Gerald Dworkin, R.G. Frey, and Sissela Bok *Euthanasia and Physician-Assisted Suicide: For and Against.* New York: Cambridge University Press, 1998.

Peter G. Filene *In the Arms of Others: A Cultural History of the Right to Die in America.* Chicago: Ivan R. Dee, 1998.

Elaine Fox et al. *Come Lovely and Soothing Death: The Right to Die Movement in the United States.* Farmington Hills, MI: Gale, 1999.

H. Leon Green *If I Should Wake Before I Die: The Medical and Biblical Truth About Near-Death Experiences.* Wheaton, IL: Crossway, 1997.

Herbert Hendin *Seduced by Death: Doctors, Patients, and the Dutch Cure.* New York: W.W. Norton, 1997.

Robert C. Horn III *How Will They Know If I'm Dead?: Transcending Disability and Terminal Illness.* Boca Raton, FL: St. Lucie, 1996.

Derek Humphry and Mary Clement *Freedom to Die: People, Politics, and the Right-to-Die Movement.* New York: St. Martin's, 1998.

John Keown, ed., and Daniel Callahan *Euthanasia Examined: Ethical, Clinical and Legal Perspectives.* New York: Cambridge University Press, 1997.

June Cerza Kolf *Comfort and Care in a Final Illness.* Tucson: Fisher, 1999.

Hans Küng et al. *Dying With Dignity: A Plea for Personal Responsibility.* New York: Continuum, 1998.

George S. Lair *Counseling the Terminally Ill: Sharing the Journey.* Washington, DC: Taylor & Francis, 1996.

Faye Landrum — *The Final Mile: A Wife's Response to Her Husband's Terminal Illness*. Wheaton, IL: Tyndale, 1999.

Edward J. Larson and Darrel W. Amundsen — *A Different Death: Euthanasia and the Christian Tradition*. Westmont, IL: InterVarsity, 1998.

Marcia Lattanzi-Licht et al. — *The Hospice Choice: In Pursuit of a Peaceful Death*. New York: Simon & Schuster, 1998.

Joanne Lynn, ed. — *Handbook for Mortals: Guidance for People Facing Serious Illness*. New York: Oxford University Press, 1999.

Michael Manning — *Euthanasia and Physician-Assisted Suicide: Killing or Caring?* Mahwah, NJ: Paulist, 1998.

Charles F. McKhann — *A Time to Die: The Place for Physician Assistance*. New Haven, CT: Yale University Press, 1999.

M. Scott Peck — *Denial of the Soul: Spiritual and Medical Perspectives on Euthanasia and Mortality*. New York: Harmony, 1997.

C.G. Prado and S.J. Taylor — *Assisted Suicide: Theory and Practice in Elective Death*. Amherst, NY: Humanity, 1999.

Timothy E. Quill — *A Midwife Through the Dying Process: Stories of Healing and Hard Choices at the End of Life*. Baltimore: Johns Hopkins University Press, 1996.

Kenneth Ring and Evelyn Elsaesser Valarino — *Lessons from the Light: What We Can Learn from the Near-Death Experience*. New York: Insight, 1998.

Betty Rollin — *Last Wish*. New York: Public Affairs, 1998.

Barbara Rommer — *Blessing in Disguise: Another Side of the Near-Death Experience*. St. Paul, MN: Llewellyn, 2000.

Lonny Shavelson — *A Chosen Death: The Dying Confront Assisted Suicide*. Berkeley: University of California Press, 1998.

Udo Schuklenk — *Access to Experimental Drugs in a Terminal Illness: Ethical Issues*. Binghamton, NY: Haworth, 1998.

Starhawk and Macha NightMare, eds. — *The Pagan Book of Living and Dying: Practical Rituals, Blessings, and Meditations on Crossing Over*. New York: HarperCollins, 1998.

Marilyn Webb — *The Good Death: The New American Search to Reshape the End of Life*. New York: Bantam, 1997.

Robert F. Weir, ed. — *Physician-Assisted Suicide*. Bloomington: Indiana University Press, 1997.

James L. Werth, ed. — *Contemporary Perspectives on Rational Suicide*. Philadelphia: Taylor & Francis, 1999.

Sue Woodman — *Last Rights: The Struggle over the Right to Die*. New York: Plenum, 1998.

Index